SUBAQUA
SWIMMING

Leo Zanelli is an author, photographer and magazine editor.
His first experience of the underwater world was in Bermuda
in 1950. The equipment he had to use at the time was not
the sort used by the modern aqualung diver, but a Dunn
helmet, which is virtually an inverted bucket with portholes.
This apparatus is placed over the head and air is pumped
through via a hose from the surface. In operation it is
delightfully simple, but it is dangerous for the inexperienced—
Leo, however, did not know that at the time.
Enthusiastic at the sights he witnessed, he spent several
years diving, using home-made equipment—the manufactured variety being almost impossible to obtain.
He joined the British Sub Aqua Club in 1958, and became
a First Class Diver in 1961. In the BSAC he became Founder
Chairman of two committees, the Accidents Committee and
the Publications Committee; eventually becoming National
Diving Officer, which is possibly the most important and
influential administrative diving position in the world.
In the latter capacity he also edited three editions of the
BSAC Diving Manual.
His great interests lie in underwater archaeology, in part-
cular shipwrecks. In fact he has written two books—
Shipwrecks Around Britain and *Unknown Shipwrecks Around
Britain*—that are divers' guides to many of the shipwrecks
of (mostly) twentieth century Britain.
He has a University of London Diploma in Archaeology,
on the subject of Palaeolithic and Mesolithic Man, and
intends to use this knowledge in investigating submerged
prehistoric caves around Britain. He is currently Editor of
Sub-Aqua Magazine, and is writing several books —all
about the underwater world.

SUBAQUA
SWIMMING

Leo Zanelli

TEACH YOURSELF BOOKS
Hodder and Stoughton

First printed 1976
Second impression 1977

Copyright © 1976
Hodder & Stoughton Ltd

ISBN O 340 20766 3

Printed and bound in Great Britain for
Hodder and Stoughton Paperbacks,
a division of Hodder and Stoughton Ltd,
Mill Road, Dunton Green, Sevenoaks, Kent,
(Editorial Office: 47 Bedford Square, London WC1 3DP)
by Elliott Bros. & Yeoman Ltd, Liverpool L24 9JL.

Contents

Foreword

The invention of the aqualung by Jacques-Yves Cousteau and Emile Gagnan in 1943 began a new era in underwater exploration and science and for the first time opened the world beneath the seas to the ordinary man and woman. Subaqua swimming is now an international recreation and pastime for the very many who find beneath the surface of sea, river and lake a new world—a world of beauty, excitement, and of never-ending interest.

The British Subaqua Club, formed in 1953 from a handful of enthusiasts, has kept pace with—and has helped set the pace for—modern techniques, equipment, and organisation, while the 'handful' of enthusiasts has now reached proportions of many thousands. It is an encouraging aspect of the British diving scene that the majority of divers belong to the BSAC; for the lone wolf, in any sphere, is seldom in a position to further its cause.

The sea is capable of extracting grave penalties from the untrained. Note that I say untrained, not inexperienced, for even an experienced underwater swimmer can make mistakes, possibly fatal, in adverse conditions—if he has not received accurate basic instruction and training. A sport that possesses even the slightest element of danger (and what really worthwhile sport does not?) cannot possess too many textbooks, providing the authors are experienced in administering instruction and have had extensive knowledge and practice of the difficulties involved. Leo Zanelli, with whom I have dived many times, fulfils these conditions, and I am very happy to extend my best wishes for the success of this book.

HAROLD GOULD
Vice-President, British Sub Aqua Club

1

The Underwater World

Why dive?

It is easy to see why underwater swimming—particularly free-diving on compressed air—is rapidly increasing in popularity, for no other sport can offer so many aspects. Quite apart from the satisfaction of achieving a certain standard of physical proficiency with training, the underwater world is the only place left on Earth where the man-in-the-street can indulge in true exploration; almost any stretch of coastline possesses underwater sites that have never been visited by man. Marine natural history has far more mystery and adventure than the land-based science, and the subaqua diver is able to witness underwater scenery, and the activities of marine life, that the expert zoologist could only guess about a few short years ago. And much remains to be discovered. Furthermore, the conscientious amateur diver is being used with greater frequency by scientists studying the underwater environment of the Continental Shelf. What, then, could be more rewarding or satisfying than an activity which combines physical skill with adventure, mystery, the thrill of exploration, and a contribution to man's knowledge of the world?

A window to the world under the sea has been opened up to everyone through the medium of cinema and television, and the exploits of Hans Hass, Cousteau and kindred souls. It is a world that most of us, with competent instruction, can visit—it is a rich experience that will stay with you for life.

A short history

Subaqua swimming is a descriptive term for underwater swimming using breathing apparatus that is independent of surface attachments. It is not a definitive term because others e.g. scuba (self-contained underwater breathing apparatus), aqualung diver, frogman, are used to describe the same activity.

The first free-diving apparatus appears to have been designed and used by a W. H. James in 1825. This consisted of a closed tunic with an integral thick leather hood that was fitted with a small glass window. The tunic was fastened at the waist and arms by elastic webbing, and air was provided by a hollow cylindrical 'belt' of iron that completely surrounded the torso from chest to hips. The air in the 'belt' was compressed to approximately thirty

CONDERT'S DIVING-APPARATUS.

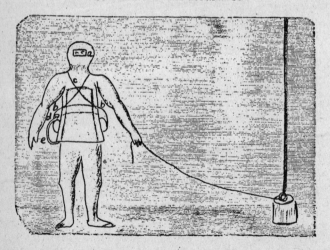

This is an ancient illustration of Condert's diving suit. The letters 'b' indicate the cylinder or tank of compressed air, 'd' the tap, and 'e' is the pipe or tube that bleeds air into the suit.

atmospheres pressure, and James is reputed to have obtained up to an hour's diving with this equipment.

Some writers have suggested that the James' apparatus was never used, and only existed in the form of drawings. Admittedly there is no concrete evidence that James actually used the equipment described, but it is worth noting that a certain Charles Condert, using a virtually identical suit, dived regularly in the East river (New York) for several months in 1832. Charles Condert died the same year, while on a dive, owing to either a malfunction of the suit or an error of technique on his part. But it is established that James' suit not only *could* have been used—but also probably was.

In 1865, Rouquayrol and Denayrouze developed a regulator that controlled a flow of air from a compressed air cylinder. This mechanism, in principle and certain details, is identical to the modern regulator or demand valve; but the lack of a suitable high-pressure cylinder rendered the regulator more suitable in conjunction with an air supply by surface hose, as used by the helmet diver.

During 1878, H. A. Fleuss, in association with Siebe, Gorman & Co., designed the first practical self-contained breathing apparatus embodying air-regenerating devices. This equipment utilized oxygen and a carbon dioxide absorbent, and was a forerunner of the Second World War equipment used by frogmen. Prior to 1914, R. H. Davis, who entered the service of Siebe, Gorman in 1882, collaborated with Fleuss in improving the apparatus; this resulted in the very reliable and efficient 'Proto' and 'Salvus' models, forms of which are still in use today.

By 1926, compressed air cylinders that could withstand a considerable pressure were available; and Commander Y. Le Prieur was experimenting with a type of Rouquayrol-Denayrouze apparatus. Although the equipment possessed certain deficiencies, by equipping the diver with fins and mask Le Prieur managed to get away from the ancient assumption that man had to walk along the sea bed. In fact Le Prieur can lay claim to being the originator of the first really free diver—one who could emulate the fish instead of plodding along the bottom with leaden feet.

During the early part of 1943, in the River Marne (France), Captain Jacques-Yves Cousteau tested a regulator designed by Emile Gagnan, an industrial gas engineer. The mechanism, in principle, had evolved from the Rouquayrol-Denayrouze regulator of the previous century. Cousteau and Gagnan modified the regulator after the first test, and this became the prototype of the modern regulator soon to be used throughout the world. Commerce was soon geared to the means of production—and the underwater world was thrown open to man on a scale that had previously been thought impossible.

A look at the future

Without doubt, much of man's future prosperity lies under the sea. The greater—and lesser—powers are expending vast sums of money on research into various aspects of the underwater world.

Off the east coast of Britain, enormous drilling barges are plunging drills through the bed of the North Sea to bring up much needed gas and oil. Off the west coast of Africa, diamonds are already being brought up in large quantities; while shallow-water dredging for tin is in operation off Indonesia.

As a source of food, the world is badly organised to benefit fully from the sea's potential, but the era of technology is changing this swiftly. Some scientists envisage underwater farms that will grow and harvest crops of seaweed and other marine plants. It is possible that certain fish could be 'herded' and domesticated; possibly electric currents or other rays could seal the estuaries of rivers, restricting the fish to a specific area. Deep water photographs have shown vast beds of manganese nodules lying on the ocean floor, awaiting the harvester.

If only a few of the forecasts become reality, a new breed will come into being—the aquanaut. Underwater houses will contain oil riggers, farmers, miners. And this is no pipe-dream; divers are already spending days and weeks researching at depth. By staying down for long periods, the diver could carry out a vast amount of work and complete underwater villages are a possibility. The working population might commute on little underwater scooters, tending plants, mining minerals or completing some other work.

The idea of man residing under the sea is climaxed by Cousteau's forecast of 'Homo Aquaticus' in which surgery —by the insertion of gills, or a regenerating oxygen cartridge installed in the body—will enable man to survive underwater for indefinite periods. This theory, startling though it might seem, has already been proved possible to some extent; laboratory tests have been carried out in which animals have existed submerged for long periods with their lungs completely filled with water.

Science has developed a membrane so thin that it will allow the passage of gases without hindrance, while still remaining completely watertight. In practice this means that one could exist underwater enclosed in a 'bubble' of skin, and while oxygen dissolved in the water could filter through the membrane, exhaled air would pass back. Artificial gills—looking something like plastic bags—have already been fashioned from this membrane and attached to breathing tubes. The human guinea-pigs testing this apparatus have used it for periods of an hour or more, obtaining their oxygen, like the fish, from the surrounding water.

All this activity will no doubt duplicate the terrestrial problems of traffic. The bathyscape has touched bottom, and taken photographs and samples, at a depth of seven miles (11·2 km). Shallow water submersibles such as Cousteau's diving saucer 'Denise' can free-range down to 1,000 feet (305 m) carrying a driver and passenger, and with a cruising time of several hours. In fact there are now literally dozens of submersibles exploring the waters of the Continental Shelf and deeper—and many of them have a cruising time measured in days rather than hours.

During the International Geophysical Year, vast areas of the Pacific were charted, and detailed study threw further light on aspects of oceanology such as current circulation, the mineral wealth of the sea bed, life cycles and population of the flora and fauna, and the mystery of certain rises and falls in sea level.

Diving and the amateur

Just a few short years ago the underwater world, although accessible by virtue of availability of equipment, was difficult for many people to visit because of the shortage of services and facilities, particularly air stations for charging cylinders. But this situation is changing rapidly. In all but the more remote parts of the world there are now sites where most facilities, including equipment hire, are available. And organized bodies such as the CMAS, NAUI, PADI, and BSAC, are making great strides in the fields of training and diving qualifications.

Because of this, you can now visit Neptune's domain, either as a spectator, viewing the scenery or taking snapshots, or as a scientist, extending the boundaries of world knowledge. The future of the underwater world is, without doubt, as exciting as the wildest science-fiction literature.

2

Getting Started

Advantages of joining a club

A basic rule—and one of the soundest—in diving is: *Never dive alone*. It's a good rule; I can remember several occasions when I have received assistance from a fellow diver, the lack of which could have had disastrous consequences. Every year there are probably several thousand unreported cases of seemingly casual help; the diver who surfaces and hands his weight belt to the surface snorkel cover because he is a little tired, or who asks for a tow. These are common occurrences, any of which could prove hazardous if the diver were solo. And all this is apart from the many reported rescues of divers in distress. So it follows that, should you need assistance of some sort, then the better trained and experienced the help available the less chance there is of disaster.

In this book my main aim is to teach you something *about* underwater swimming. Attempting to teach yourself is only asking for trouble, and I advise that actual underwater experience and training is only carried out under the supervision of a qualified diving instructor.

The most important attribute of a good diving club is the provision of training facilities and adequate instruction. Experienced members can provide advice and a fund of available knowledge. Occasionally, equipment can be hired or borrowed, enabling you to experiment a little before buying your own. Courses of lectures on diving are given, and attendance is often a necessity, as they form part of the training. The social side of a club is also important, and consists of 'dry' (as distinct from swimming) meetings. Here, apart from enabling you to talk diving, a film show or lecture by a prominent diving authority is often held. Apart from all this, a club will have a planned diving programme. This consists of various grades of diving, some suitable for beginners, others for the more proficient diver, arranged well in advance and enabling you to fit in the type of dive most suited to your standard of experience.

Throughout the world, clubs form a pool of diving information for local areas. Clubs have been instrumental in instituting safe diving techniques and campaigning against laws that could be unfair to underwater swimmers. Many clubs contain groups that are active in the fields of underwater photography, archaeology, biology and other aspects of the underwater world. They also provide, in many cases, a service to the community by assisting the police and local authorities with searches and information.

Diving on your own or with inexperienced partners is dangerous. Diving with a club you can have much more fun, and improve your knowledge, in relative safety.

Importance of steam swimming

'Steam' swimming—that is, ordinary swimming without artificial aids such as fins—is an important adjunct to preliminary diving training. It is quite true that most non-swimmers get on quite well in the water if equipped with fins and mask, but a good standard in steam swimming develops a healthy attitude towards water in general. A competent swimmer will usually develop into a confident diver, because watermanship is the first essential in preventing that most dangerous swimming hazard—panic. It is difficult to set a standard of swimming from which to progress to aqualung training, and most authorities have different tests—but they all agree that a swimming test is desirable. And in most clubs and for most diving courses, the passing of a swimming test is essential before you are allowed to graduate to aqualung use.

To start with, a good swimmer should be capable of a variety of strokes: crawl, breast, and a back stroke. Utilizing any of these strokes you should be able to swim 300 metres in nine minutes or less. After that, swim an additional 100 metres wearing a 5 kilo weight belt (before you do this, check that you are neutrally buoyant without the belt, by taking a deep breath, curling yourself into a ball and floating in the water. If you can't float like this, use less weight on the belt).

The ability to float, motionless—or with a minimum of hand movement, is a sign of good watermanship. It is not necessary to learn the difficult horizontal float, a vertical float held for several minutes indicates confidence and ability.

An exercise often introduced into swimming tests is treading water with the hands held above the head. Normally, a swimmer finds treading water quite easy, but when the hands are raised above the head the effect is to push the head under. A quick, light, breast stroke action is required of the legs to complete this exercise, and you should be able to keep it up for around one minute. I have never been quite convinced of the necessity of this exercise, having seen some excellent swimmers spend an awful lot of time mastering it, but this is an academic point if your club or course requires it.

A good jack-knife surface dive to the bottom of the pool to recover an object weighing about 5 kilos will, when perfected, ensure that no trouble is experienced when you graduate to this same dive in the snorkelling tests.

At this stage remember that is it perfectly natural for the novice to want to rush on to aqualung training as soon as possible; bothering to brush up on your swimming techniques, and spending your time fin swimming, can be tiresome when all that gleaming equipment lies by the side of the pool. But bear in mind that when you are diving you

hold two lives in your hands—your own and your partner's—
and you each have the right to expect a certain standard
of competence in the other.

Importance of a medical examination

Although underwater swimming is a health-promoting
sport, it can prove dangerous if your physical or medical
fitness is in doubt. Taking the various stresses into account
(the loss of body heat and energy owing to the lower
temperature of the water, the high oxygen consumption,
and the effects of pressure—even now not fully understood),
it is easy to see why it is advisable that a medical examination should precede starting underwater swimming.

Your doctor might be a little hazy as to what, exactly, is
required—quite understandably: this is a relatively new
sport, and you must be of some assistance to him. Some
afflictions spell obvious danger: heart disease, pulmonary
tuberculosis, fits, asthma, and any weakening disease. Less
obvious, at least from the non-diver's point of view, are
ear troubles, sinus problems, and any tendency towards
headaches. Some people suffer occasional attacks of
giddiness or fainting without ever bothering to consult
their doctor, but even if the giddiness is mild and infrequent,
the cause should be checked.

A medical examination is for your own good—and the
good of your future 'buddy' divers. Exhaustion, fainting and
vomiting are all distressing enough on land; under water
they can be fatal.

If you have a diving club near you, then in all probability
they will know of a doctor who specializes, or at least takes
an interest, in diving. If so, then use the diving doctor for
your medical examination.

The mask

The mask is really the one essential in underwater swimming. The haunting beauty of the underwater world and the mechanical efficiency of the regulator would go unappreciated and unused if man were blind under water—and he is! It is the mask that gives us the magic facility of sight under water; all other subaqua equipment merely serves to extend the range and application of the mask.

The reasons for the mask unblurring man's vision under water are given in the section on physics, and need not be repeated here. However, we do need to know something about the construction, design and function of masks to assist us in selecting a suitable model.

First of all, goggles should never be worn for underwater swimming. A good mask should cover both eyes and nose. The reason for this is that as the swimmer descends the pocket of air in goggles or mask compresses, creating a dangerous squeeze on the eyeballs. This problem can easily be overcome if you can breathe into the mask through your nose; but this is impossible with goggles, which cover only the eyes. Also, water in the mask can be cleared by a good snort into the mask—again impossible with goggles.

Having eliminated goggles, we can also dispose of another type of mask—the full-face version that covers eyes, nose and mouth. This type is manufactured with built-in snorkel tubes with one-way valves on the ends; the whole assembly gives its owner a fearsome appearance. Don't even contemplate this kind. A full-face mask makes it impossible to use the underwater breathing apparatus normally available. Also, it is difficult to get off if it floods. The built-in snorkels are equipped with various valves to prevent water getting into the mask when its owner submerges, but snorkel valves have been vetoed by authorities all over the world as being of little use—and sometimes a positive danger.

When selecting a mask, choose a model that covers your eyes and nose. Place the mask on your face, with the straps hanging free, and inhale gently through your nose; if the fit is good, the mask will stay on your face by the suction alone. Probably many masks will pass this test, and in this case buy the one which feels most comfortable.

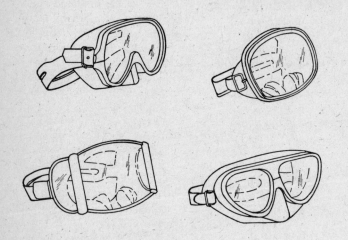

A selection of masks from the Scubapro range. They all have facilities for pinching the nostrils, and the one for you is merely a question of preference, comfort and fit.

The transparent front window or face plate can be of plastic, which is tougher and safer than glass, but which also has the disadvantages of continually misting up and scratching easily. Most good face plates are made in toughened glass; a sandblasted mark to this effect should be present somewhere on the surface. Some face plates are manufactured from laminated glass (a layer of plastic sandwiched between two layers of glass with special adhesive). This is an excellent material, but you should ensure that the laminate is not separating at the edges. This can be checked by examining the edge surface of the plate, which means you will have to dismantle the holding band round the plate—a procedure likely to be discouraged by the salesman!

Some of the cheaper masks actually use ordinary glass for the face plate. The ease with which this can break or shatter, and the dangers involved, need no stressing. Sufficient to say that on no account—even financial—should face plates of ordinary glass be worn.

Occasionally you will find a mask with a yellow-tinted face plate. The theory is that yellow increases the contrast and 'sharpens' the vision. No doubt this theory can be proved on a test bench, but it is difficult to see this improvement with the naked eye. The tinting does alter the colour rendering of the water, particularly at shallow depths, and some people prefer this, but they are in an extremely small minority.

An innovation in the standard mask that has proved its worth is the facility to enable you to grasp or pinch your nose to seal off the nostrils. This usually consists of depressions in the mask, one outside each nostril. The reason for this is that some people cannot 'clear' their ears without pinching their nostrils and blowing gently (this may sound odd, but is explained in the snorkel diving section), so the purchase of a mask with ear clearing facilities depends on the ease with which you can clear your ears. Most divers wisely purchase a mask with this facility, because your physical condition can vary from day to day, and even the diver with 'clear' ears can, for no obvious reason, experience difficulty on some days.

Another innovation, a built-in purge valve for clearing the mask of any accumulated water, is a luxury device. It works out cheaper to roll on your back or side and clear the water the orthodox way (also explained later). Furthermore, a valve introduces a mechanical element to a very simple article—just something else to go wrong.

The holding strap of a mask should be of 'split-band' design. This, in effect, branches out into two bands at the rear of the head resulting in a safer, more comfortable and more secure fitting.

Fins or flippers

Without fins the underwater swimmer would be an ungainly individual, probably descending with the aid of lead ballast and ascending with a form of buoyancy bag. Fins allow the diver to move through the water with a flexible ease, leaving his hands free to perform other tasks. The hands, incidentally, are sometimes used to aid balance, but never to assist propulsion. Underwater arm movement would only slow you down.

Comfort is the first consideration in selecting your fins. A loose flipper will chafe and cause blisters—if it stays on—while one that is too tight will restrict circulation and cause cramp. When purchasing, bear in mind whether the fins will be used on bare feet or over the bootees of a wet or dry suit; there will be a difference of several sizes.

Broadly, there are two types of fin, one with a full foot fitting and the other with an open heel that is held on by straps.

The most popular are the full foot fitting; these transform the fin into an integral part of the leg and, if the fit is correct, are safer. The open heel and strap type is usually cheaper but the point where the fin meets the foot can chafe. Also, if a strap breaks the diver is helpless unless he knows how to swim the dolphin stroke. Strangely, one of the most expensive fins has an open heel and strap fitting, but this is because it is a large competition fin and a full foot moulding would make it even more expensive.

Black fins are usually made from a heavy, rigid rubber. Coloured types are usually more pliable and often float, which can be an advantage.

The blade area of a fin is important. Although a large blade provides powerful propulsion on the feet of a swimmer with strong, fit legs, this can prove exhausting to an ordinary mortal; the average swimmer is better off with a fin of moderate surface area. The same is true of the rigidity of the fin blade. A rigid blade may be faster but it requires a great deal of effort. The flexible blade is slower but easier on the legs.

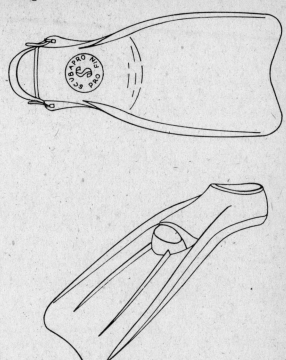

Two types of fins from the Scubapro range. The full foot fitting fin (lower) is the most popular and safest for the average diver. The fin with the heel strap is designed for the professional; it has a large blade area and provides powerful propulsion—but you could be in trouble if a strap breaks.

Fin retainers are 'Y'-shaped rubber straps which are slipped over the fin and ankle to prevent the fins from slipping off. Because a diver could be in trouble over the loss of a fin, fin retainers are useful accessories that should be worn whenever possible. They are only of value with full foot fitting fins; they won't hold the open heel and strap variety on.

Snorkel

The basic equipment of a skin diver consists, essentially, of just mask and fins, but the snorkel tube has proved such a practical success that it is now considered as part of a skin diver's basic equipment. In fact the term 'snorkeling' is now taken to mean just skin diving—that is, underwater swimming with just fins, mask and snorkel.

In use, a snorkel allows the user to breathe easily while swimming on the surface of the water face down. This eliminates the tiresome and exhausting necessity of continually raising the head in order to breathe. It is also invaluable to the aqualung diver in very many instances; when the diver has no air left in his cylinder yet still has to swim back, or if he just wishes to conserve air while on the surface. Most responsible, well-trained divers carry a snorkel tube as part of their standard equipment.

Basically a snorkel is a straight—or slightly curved—tube with a 'U' bend at one end, and to which is fitted a mouthpiece. Some snorkels are fitted with one-way valves that prevent water entering the tube while underwater. These are not only unnecessary but possibly dangerous. The snorkel with a plain, open end requires very little practice to use properly, and is an uncomplicated design with no moving parts to go wrong.

In theory, a snorkel tube with a large bore or diameter is difficult, even impossible, to clear water from (also explained later), and a tube that is too long is undesirable because of the excessive amount of exhaled air that would be re-inhaled. In fact, no snorkels sold in a shop would provide tubes with such specifications.

When selecting your snorkel, pay especial attention to the mouthpiece and the angle of curve in the U-bend. The mouthpiece must be comfortable at all times, and the U-bend should have sufficient curve to enable you to wear the snorkel with the mouthpiece flush with your mouth.

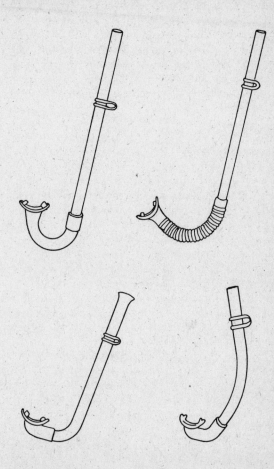

A selection of snorkels from the US Divers range. They are all recommended—the one you choose is a question of preference.

This needs explaining. Some U-bends have short, tight curves, which means that the mouthpiece is quite close to the tube itself, and in this case the arrangement would suit someone with a small face. Conversely, a U-bend with a wide sweep is more suitable for larger faces.

Snorkels are usually fitted—indeed should be fitted—with a retaining ring that holds the snorkel tube onto the mask strap at the side of the head. Whether you wear the tube on the right or left side of your head, inside or outside the strap, is a matter of preference.

Nose clips and ear plugs

Underwater swimmers should not need their noses held closed by artificial devices. The nostrils should be open for equalizing pressure and clearing water from the mask. One argument in favour of nose clips says that they are useful in case the mask is accidentally dislodged, in which case the nose is in contact with water. The fault in this argument is that the nose clip will probably also be dislodged if a mask is knocked off. You should practice finning along the surface of the pool, face down and without a mask, breathing through a snorkel. Most people find this almost impossible at first, but you should be 'O.K'. by the third or fourth attempt. If it doesn't come easily, persevere until it does, because then you will be quite safe in the water if your mask is knocked off.

Ear plugs are of no use whatsoever to underwater swimmers. Although possibly of some use to surface swimmers, under water the pressure would drive the ear plugs into the ear itself and cause considerable damage.

Snorkel diving: the basic techniques

Let us imagine you are by the side of a swimming pool, ready to try out your new equipment for the first time.

Sit on the edge of the pool and put your fins on. Next

take hold of your mask, spit on the inside of the face plate and rub the spittle evenly all over the inside surface, then rinse the mask out in the water. This treatment will prevent the face plate from misting up when you are under water.

If your snorkel is already attached to the mask strap, then place the mouthpiece in your mouth; if your snorkel does not have a retaining ring, then slide the tube under the mask strap before popping the opposite end in your mouth.

Now slide into the water and hang on to the side or, better still, a ladder; as you do this, keep your face in the water, observing the underwater scene around you, and getting used to breathing through the snorkel. When you feel quite comfortable, release your hold and swim a couple of lengths. At first your legs will tend to make a bicycling action, but try to avoid this; try to keep your knees reasonably rigid, your hands held next to your sides, and don't let your fins break the water and thrash around in the air—not even your heels.

The next step is to learn how to clear your snorkel. Stand in the pool in the shallow end at a point where the water reaches your chest. Now either lean forward or bend your knees until your snorkel is completely under water; straighten up, and blow sharply to clear the water. The first few attempts may make you cough, but persevere. The inhalation immediately after clearing the tube should be a smooth, gentle one. If you 'snatch' (that is, inhale sharply), you may inhale a few drops of water trapped in the U-bend, making you cough and ruining the effort.

As has been mentioned, a mask that comes off—perhaps by an accidental knock or a strap snapping—is a great danger to the untrained diver. This is because there is a tendency to breathe through your nose when this happens. When mastered, the following exercise will ensure, in the event that of such a mishap occurring, that you will remain calm and competent.

Retire to one end of the pool, remove your mask and leave it on the side of the pool. Now swim a length, face down, breathing through your snorkel (you will have to hold the snorkel in place at the U-bend, otherwise it will dip into the water). Do not pinch your nostrils shut with your free hand, and keep your eyes open. It is a good plan to follow one of the black lines that usually run the length of the pool because your blurred vision will see little else. This exercise is invaluable training and must be mastered. If you find it difficult at first, don't try for too long because the chemicals in the water will make your eyes bloodshot. Even after you have mastered this procedure, it is wise to give it a run through once in a while—say a couple of times a year.

When you are quite happy snorkelling without your mask, you are ready to attempt mask clearing. If your mask does come off underwater, and you recover it, it will be necessary to clear it of water; but it's more than likely it will be only a slight leak. The method of clearing is the same in both cases.

Go to the ladder at the deep end, leaving your fins and snorkel at the side of the pool. Half-fill your mask with water and put it on. Take a deep breath through your mouth and submerge by climbing down the ladder. While holding on securely with one hand (left hand if you are right-handed, and vice versa) and both feet, to prevent yourself floating back to the surface. Tilt your head so that you are looking at the surface of the water, place your free hand along the top of the mask and press gently—now blow firmly and steadily through your nose.

What happens—or what should happen!—is this: as you breathe into the mask the air, being lighter than water, rises and accumulates at the top of the mask; it cannot escape because your hand is holding the top of the mask firmly against your forehead. As more air is released into the mask, it occupies more and more space, driving the water steadily downwards through the bottom or 'loose' end of the mask. When only air bubbles through the bottom of the mask, it is completely cleared.

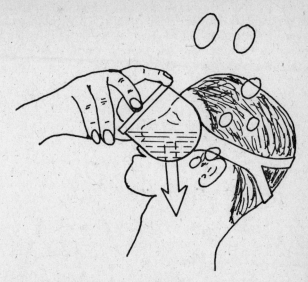

Clearing water from the mask. The top of the mask is held firmly, pressing it gently against the forehead. Air is blown out through the nose; the air can not escape through the top as it normally would, so it expands downwards, pushing the water out of the mask.

Once you have the hang of it—and it is essential that you do—you will find that you do not require an explosion of bubbles to clear your mask. The well-trained diver should be able to clear a fully flooded mask at least three times on a single lungful of air.

When you can clear half a mask of water, try the same exercise but this time take a deep breath, submerge, flood your mask fully, then clear.

Whether aqualung or snorkel diving, you should always adjust your weight belt so that you are slightly buoyant at the surface. This, however, poses a minor problem when you attempt to submerge; a little downward thrust is required, and this is provided by your legs in the following manner. Snorkel along the surface, take a light breath, plunge the top part of your body downwards, as if you were trying to touch your toes; at the same time, throw both your legs

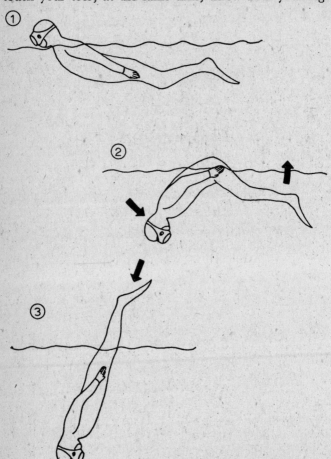

Sequence of a clean surface or jack-knife dive.

up into the air; the weight of your legs will push you neatly underwater with scarcely a splash if you have performed the action—a jack-knife surface dive—correctly.

While practising the surface dive you may note, at a certain depth, a pressure or ache in your ear-drum. The cause is explained in the section on physics; at this stage we are more concerned how to eliminate this discomfort.

The various methods of alleviating or preventing pressure on the ear-drums are all known as 'clearing the ears', and whatever method you use should be applied as soon as there is any sign of pressure; don't wait until the onset of pain because you could easily tear an ear-drum.

There are three methods to try initially, these being suitable for people whose ears are relatively easy to clear, and these consist of swallowing, pretending to yawn, or snorting into your mask. If you are one of the fortunates who can clear their ears by one of the above methods, then fine, but experiment a little to find which one suits you best. Should none of these actions have any effect—and this is usually the case—attempt the following procedure: seal your nostrils (this is where the mask designed for this facility comes in) by squeezing them together, and try to blow gently through your nose, that is, against your sealed nostrils. If this does not work try waggling your jaws as you try to blow. Don't blow very hard, even if you find it a little difficult, because you could damage your ear-drum.

If none of these methods succeed in clearing your ears, there are several possible explanations. You might be suffering from a cold (in which case you shouldn't be in the water), or catarrh might be blocking certain vital passages or tubes. In any case, don't try to 'force' your ears, leave it and try again another day. Should you still have no success after several attempts (several days, that is), then consult your doctor.

Keeping in trim is an important aspect of any sport, and particularly underwater swimming. If you frequent a swimming pool regularly, and you should if one is available, don't spend your time aimlessly splashing around; the following exercise, when mastered, combines watermanship with technique and stamina, an ideal worth aiming at.

Basically the exercise is a combination of techniques, and consists of sinking your fins, mask and snorkel in the pool at a depth of around two metres; diving down and fitting them on while underwater, clearing the mask at the same time; clearing the snorkel on surfacing; and finning a fast 200 metres, performing a jack-knife or surface dive to the bottom each time you are in the deep end.

Of course, fitting all basic equipment underwater on a single breath should not be attempted initially. Take the items one by one at first. Sink all the equipment, then dive down for the mask, clearing it before you surface; tread water for a few minutes to regain your breathing rhythm before diving for the snorkel, clearing the snorkel on surfacing; and tread water again until ready to dive for your fins, fitting them on underwater. Gradually, with practice, you will be able to complete two articles with one dive, and then all three. Note that this is not a breath-holding competition—that would require careful super-vision. So if you fumble an article, don't stay underwater until your lungs feel as if they could burst—come up, rest, and try again. Similarly, don't practise until you are ready to drop.

When you have mastered this exercise, get into the habit of fitting your basic equipment under water, and complete a good surface swim every time you visit the pool, as a preliminary to anything else you might have lined up.

3

Physics and Medical

Most people recoil at the mere mention of physics, but little more than basic arithmetic is required for the information presented here, and the diver needs a certain amount of knowledge regarding the laws relating to, and the composition of, air and water in order to understand the problems of buoyancy adjustment, decompression, embolism, ear-clearing, and the various ailments that a liquid environment can create. It is important, therefore, not to gloss over this chapter. The information that pressure is doubled at a depth of 33 feet or 10 metres may not sound as exciting as the location of a wreck, but it is of greater importance to the diver who wishes to reach a ripe old age.

Effects of pressure

The atmospheric air we breathe consists of a variety of gases: approximately 78% nitrogen, 21% oxygen, 1% argon, less than 0·4% carbon dioxide, and smaller quantities of other gases. This air is virtually held in place by the gravitational pull of the Earth, and at sea level exerts a pressure termed 'one atmosphere' (14·7 pounds per square inch in pre-metric terms). This pressure is exerted equally from all directions and the human body has become adjusted to it; indeed it is not normally noticed until a malfunction such as a heavy cold or sinus trouble occurs.

Air is compressible. Thus, by virtue of its own pressure or

'weight' it gets progressively denser as it nears sea level. For example, although it exerts a pressure of one atmosphere (or 'at') at sea level, the pressure at the top of Mount Everest is less than one third of an atmosphere. It is this compressibility that enables the aqualung diver to invade the deep; a vast quantity of air can be forced into a cylinder, providing the diver with a portable quantity of air.

Water is 800 times more dense than air—$0 \cdot 0283$ m³ (one cubic foot) of sea water weighs approximately 29 kg or 64 pounds—and is virtually incompressible. This means that the water at the bottom of the ocean is no denser than that near the surface, and that the enormous pressures existing at the bottom are the result of the sheer weight of the water above. The difference in density is shown by the fact that a layer of air many miles thick produces a pressure of one atmosphere, yet to double this pressure under water requires a depth of only 10 metres or 33 feet.

Pressure under water is usually expressed in standard units of atmospheres—or sometimes 'bars', which are for all practical purposes identical. There are two methods of using underwater pressure calculations: 'gauge' pressure, which ignores the pressure of atmospheric air and indicates the pressure of water only, and 'absolute', which includes the unit of one atmosphere existing at sea level. A diver at a depth of 10 metres would thus be subject to a pressure of one atmosphere gauge or two atmospheres (or bars) absolute. In diving, an otherwise unqualified calculation is assumed to read absolute.

The human body is composed of virtually incompressible fluids and solids, and is relatively unaffected by pressure provided that the pressure has access to all the body surfaces—and there's the rub. The body has a number of internal cavities (lungs, sinus spaces, inner ear spaces) and if pressure is applied to the body externally—as when swimming under water on a single breath with no aqualung —these cavities are subjected to a compressive effect which can, in certain circumstances, cause pain and damage.

What is required is the introduction into these cavities of a pressure that will equal the external pressure of water; and this is where the cylinder of compressed air comes in.

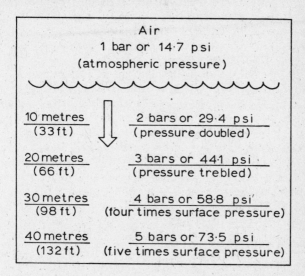

Showing the increase in pressure as the diver descends.

At a depth of 20 metres, a diver has a pressure of three atmospheres absolute pressing all over his external surfaces. As he sucks on his mouthpiece, his regulator will regulate the flow of air from his cylinder at this same pressure. Provided the diver has no ailment such as a cold, this compressed air will flood the internal cavities, compensating the external pressure, and no discomfort will be felt. Such is the miracle of the regulator.

Breathing compressed air is not without its complications (these are described in the medical section) but they all derive from the following facts or laws: at a depth of 10 metres or 33 feet, a diver receives air, through his regulator, that is compressed to a pressure of two atmospheres absolute—double the pressure breathed at sea level—to compensate for the ambient or surrounding water pressure. At this moment the diver's lungs contain twice the amount of air (in compressed form, although this air takes up the same amount of space) as would normally be breathed at sea level. This means that the lungs, at his depth, contain twice as much oxygen, nitrogen, carbon dioxide etc. Deeper, at 20 metres or 66 feet, the diver breathes air compressed to three atmospheres, with a proportionate increase of the gases in the air. The deeper the dive, the higher the compression of air that is delivered through the regulator, and the greater the intake of the gases that the air consists of. These gases reach every part of the body, and it is this bodily 'saturation' of gases, and/or the expansion of this compressed air when the diver rises to the surface, that can give rise to nitrogen narcosis, embolism and other subaquatic ailments.

Vision under water

The human eye is adapted for use in air, not water. Consequently, if you open your eyes, and they are in contact with the water, they will be severely out of focus and able to judge only light and shade. Everything else will be blurred. But if a pocket of air is placed between the eyes and the water, such as when a mask is being worn, then the eyes will be working in contact with air once again, and can function virtually as well as normal.

But there is still a difference. Water has what is called a higher refractive index than air, which means that when the eye looks through water in this fashion, the water has a magnifying effect. In practice, this means that objects viewed through a face mask, while under water, appear to be approximately one third nearer than they usually are. With most people this illusion throws their judgement of distance slightly out for the first few times a mask is worn, but the brain soon adjusts to this condition and this particular effect rarely causes any problem.

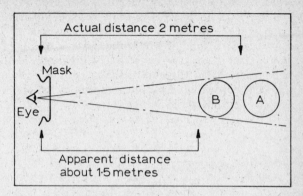

Underwater, everything appears to be nearer than it really is. But the eye soon gets used to it.

Water is denser than air—800 times more so, in fact—and because of this it absorbs light to a greater degree than air does, and it also acts as a light reducing filter. This means that underwater visibility and brightness is never as good as it is at the surface.

Added to this is the fact that water, because of its density, is able to hold quite large pieces of sediment suspended in it. No doubt you have noticed how well mud mixes with water! This sediment actually forms a barrier to vision, cutting down the visibility and screening out the light. Consequently, if the sediment is thick enough, you will only be able to see a few centimetres or inches, and it will be dark at quite shallow depths.

Another peculiarity of water is that it absorbs colours, doing this most effectively at the red/orange end of the spectrum. Take a red object underwater, and at 3 metres depth it will appear to be a very ordinary brown. At about 10 metres the red will have virtually disappeared. Deeper than 20 metres everything underwater has a blue or green—depending on the colour of the water itself—cast, with no trace whatsoever of reds, oranges or yellows, even though those colours may be present. However, the colour may be seen, whatever the depth, if you use some form of artificial lighting such as a torch. This is usually the reason why underwater photographers use artificial lighting such as flash when there is no apparent shortage of light; they use the supplementary lighting to bring out the colours present. The illustration shows this more clearly.

Colours fade as the diver descends. But if artificial light, such as a torch or floodlight, is introduced, this will reveal the original or real colours.

Sound under water

If the diver removes his mouthpiece while underwater, and attempts to talk, the result is an unintelligible gabble. Although sound travels at around 300 metres per second in air, and five times faster in water, their physical differences are such as to prevent transmission of the greater part of sound through air and into water, and vice versa. As the diver's words originate in the medium of air (the throat), they are nullified at the air/water demarcation line after they leave the mouth.

But the underwater world is not completely silent. The diver can utilize sound by striking two hard surfaces for simple signals. Two rocks in contact will produce a clicking noise that can be heard over a considerable distance, as can the ringing sound produced by tapping a cylinder with an object such as a knife handle. Sound produced in this manner can be developed into a quite sophisticated set of signals if required.

Exhaustion

Of the many dangerous conditions and ailments that can befall the subaqua diver, exhaustion is undoubtedly the most common. Luckily, only a small percentage of divers ever suffer the bends, narcosis, or other exotic-sounding disorders, but every underwater swimmer experiences, at some time or other, the hazard of fatigue.

There are many causes of exhaustion, including panic, cold, and over-exertion, but they can all be reduced as a potential danger by careful planning and regular training. One of the main causes, without doubt, is overweighting. A long swim home can be tiring at the end of a dive, and it is here, on the surface and out of cylinder air, that the diver is most vulnerable. If the diver is too heavy on the surface on the long swim back, his snorkel will drop lower and lower into the water until a mouthful of water is inhaled—then panic. On the surface, a diver should be weighted so that he is neutrally buoyant (this means that he sinks as he exhales and rises as he inhales) when he is fully equipped with fully charged cylinders. This means that when he returns he will be lighter because he will have used some air up (the air in the cylinders adds to the weight) and will float on the surface.

Although fins give the underwater swimmer greater power, even this method of propulsion will create little impression against a fast current. If things go wrong, and you have to battle your way out of a swift flow, don't attempt to swim directly against the current; swim across it in a diagonal direction.

Like most things, the regulator is not perfect; there is a fractional time lag that is not noticed in normal use, but when over exertion causes heavy breathing, a stage can be reached when insufficient air is being supplied. In this condition, the diver should, if possible, cease all movement and relax. Try to get into a position where the regulator is below the level of the chest. This will have the effect of increasing the air flow in the case of twin hose regulators. If a single hose regulator is being used, the purge valve might need activating. The important thing is to try to restore a normal breathing rythmn.

Cold and fatigue go hand in hand, and are dealt with in the sections of Diving Under Ice and Protective Clothing.

It is impossible to tell whether a person would, or would not, panic under certain circumstances or conditions, but it is possible to cut the chances down. A well-trained diver is more likely to go through procedure automatically in an emergency, so don't fall out of practice with the drills; use your local swimming pool for constant revision and training. It only needs one emergency and a life saved— possibly yours—to have made it all worth while.

Ears and sinus

A diver usually has one particular physical indication that he is being subjected to above-average pressure; the sensation in his ears, or, more correctly, the middle ear space. To understand this condition correctly, a basic knowledge of the ear and hearing mechanism is required.

Basically, the ear is divided into three parts; the outer ear, which is the fleshy 'bit that sticks out' and includes the canal that leads to the ear drum; the middle ear, which lies beyond the ear drum and consists of an air space with a tube—the Eustachian tube—leading to the throat; and another drum, which connects to the internal ear where all the hearing 'works' are located.

Briefly, sound travels along the outer ear canal, and vibrations echo across the middle ear space (some light bones assist here) to the internal ear, where hearing takes place.

The Eustachian tube is the only contact that the middle ear has with atmospheric air, and one of its functions is to keep the air pressure in this chamber adjusted properly. If the Eustachian tube in normal use becomes blocked or closed, through catarrh or swollen membranes, the middle ear space becomes sealed off. The air inside is slowly absorbed through surrounding tissue and the pressure in the space drops below atmospheric; the outer ear drum is then subject to a pressure that is higher on the outside, resulting in ear-ache—a common pain when you have a cold.

In diving, this problem is magnified and speeded up: pressure changes so abruptly that the Eustachian tube can be forced shut at its narrow end (at the throat), isolating the middle ear space. On descending, the rapidly increasing external pressure causes pain and, if the descent continues with a closed Eustachian tube, the ear drum could puncture or tear. Fortunately, the average person can perform a simple ear-clearing action: a few can do this by pretending to yawn with the mouth closed; but usually this is inadequate, and more often the nostrils are pinched or held closed, and a *gentle* blow attempted through the nose against the closed nostrils. This should have the effect of forcing the Eustachian open. But don't overdo it—too hard a blow and you could burst your ear drum outwards! Both, or either, of these actions should open the Eustachian tube and must be carried out when the slightest pressure is felt—don't wait until the onset of pain. In fact, an experienced diver will clear instinctively as he descends, even before pressure is actually felt

Should an ear drum perforate, there are various symptoms. The most dangerous aspect is when water trickles through the perforation; apart from the possibility of infection, cold water in the inner ear can cause sickness, dizziness, and a complete loss of the sense of balance. In this case, the diver will not even know the direction of the surface and should, if possible, grab hold of something solid. When the water in the inner ear has warmed up to body temperature, the sense of balance will return. However, if you should ever be in this condition and you feel the hands of your buddy holding you, he is probably bringing you to the surface, so don't struggle or hold your breath (see Air embolism).

Other symptoms of a perforated ear drum are: bubbles escaping from the ear (this can quite definitely be felt), in which case get out of the water fast; or a discharge of blood from the ear, with or without pain.

In all cases the ear should be covered—not plugged—with an antiseptic cloth or lint, and a doctor seen as soon as possible. Provided there are no complications, a small puncture will often heal within several days, but keep out of the water until the doctor gives you the O.K.

The human skull has several natural air spaces (sinuses) located within its frontal section. Their function is dubious and outside the scope of this book, but they can create a problem almost identical to that of the inner ear. The sinuses have connections (named ostia) through to the nose, and these perform the same function as the Eustachian tube. When the ostia are blocked, the air pressure in the respective sinus cannot equalize and severe pain will be felt on descending, and a little blood might be discharged into the mask. Note that sinuses *cannot* be cleared while on a dive; if pain is felt, diving should be abandoned for the day. A cold is probably the cause—in which case diving should never have even started. In the event of a sinus condition persisting for several days, a doctor should be consulted.

In any event, *never* dive if you have a cold, stuffy nose, or a chill, however slight.

Drinking

There are two types of liquid refreshment that can affect a diver's performance or condition adversely. The most obvious is alcohol. The effects of intoxicants such as alcohol while the body is subjected to pressure have not been fully investigated, but there is evidence that even residual alcohol—the stuff still around the morning after—can seriously impair the diver's performance, and perhaps even make him more susceptible to nitrogen narcosis. Little need be said about the befuddling mental action experienced as the result of alcohol, and the potential danger to the diver. So it you're drinking, don't dive—and go easy the night before you do.

Of more subtle danger is the carbonated 'fizzy' drink. A sparkling drink will not fizz while in a sealed bottle, being restrained by the pressure built up in the small air space. Should a diver consume a carbonated drink before diving, the pressure, while underwater, will tend to subdue the drink, and none of those disconcerting burps will occur—that is, until the diver surfaces. Then, as the pressure reduces, the 'fizz' will be released. By this time, the liquid may have travelled far in its journey to the bladder, and pockets of carbonated gases will form, sometimes causing severe discomfort. Sparkling drinks of any type should not be consumed for at least two hours before a dive. And remember, sparkling drinks include beer or sparkling wine such as champagne, even if it is 'only the one'. In any case, they contain alcohol . . .

Cramp

Cramp is a painful spasm of a muscle, or group of muscles, usually affecting the lower limbs, although stomach cramp is not uncommon. It is of greater danger to the steam swimmer than the diver, unless the latter is on the surface, out of air and overweighted—a situation he should not get into. The spasm may last a few seconds or several minutes, and can be brought on by exertion, cold, or working in a confined or awkward position. A meal eaten before a dive can divert blood to the abdominal organs, leaving the muscles in the arms and legs relatively short of blood and liable to cramp.

If cramp occurs, stretch the limb and rub the affected part if possible; and get out of the water as soon as you can. When out of the water, massage the area and, if the cramp persists, apply heat if available.

Air embolism

From the section on physics, we know that a diver at any depth has more than the usual quantity of air compressed into his lungs, to compensate for the increased ambient or surrounding pressure. When a diver ascends, the water pressure decreases, and the compressed air in the lungs expands. Should a diver ascend rapidly, or while holding his breath, the pressure in the lungs becomes greater than the external water pressure, in effect over-expanding the lungs; in this situation, air may be forced into the lung walls, forming bubbles that can enter the circulation, blocking and rupturing small blood vessels. Prevention is better than cure, so always ascend at a steady pace; the inhalation should be short and the exhalation long. If it should become necessary to surface rapidly—an air failure for example—keep your mouth and throat open (it is possible to do one and not the other) and let the air flow out. When you are near the surface, say the last 7 metres

(20 feet) or so, breathe out fast. Panic *can* cause the throat to seize up, preventing the air from escaping freely; but if this occurs, it is usually the result of poor or inadequate training.

The symptoms of an embolism are many: hoarse throat or chest, muzzy speech, tight chest, dizzyness, blood or froth from the mouth, numbness or paralysis of the extremities, unconsciousness, convulsions. There is no first aid treatment that can be applied on the spot. Keep the subject warm and rush him to the nearest recompression chamber. Speed is of vital importance; a few minutes can make all the difference between life and death.

Another hazard is spontaneous pneumothorax, which is the result of air being trapped between the chest and the lung. On ascent, the expanding air can collapse the lung and even displace the heart. Symptoms include pains in the chest, extreme shortness of breath, irregular pulse, and dark discolouration of the skin around the chest. Immediate medical treatment is essential, because this might entail puncturing the chest with a needle to release the air, something that should not be attempted by the layman.

Decompression sickness

Of all the diving illnesses, this could be called the most 'glamorous', it certainly receives a lot of publicity in the popular Press. The 'bends', or decompression sickness, derives its name from the contorted positions that its crippling pain forces a sufferer to adopt. More divers, particularly professionals, have been maimed or killed by the bends than by any other diving hazard.

The basic cause is a condition termed nitrogen absorption. A diver breathing compressed air will be absorbing an above-average concentration of each gas that the air is composed of. In the case of nitrogen, the excess will normally dissolve in the blood as the diver ascends, and is breathed out through the lungs. However, should a diver exceed a certain depth for a prolonged period of time, the body absorbs nitrogen to a level at which the following condition can occur.

As the diver rises to the surface, the excess nitrogen may come out of solution faster than the blood can carry it away, forming small bubbles in the tissues and the blood. These bubbles can lodge in almost any part of the body, causing the severe pain that gives rise to the bends. The medical treatment is to recompress the bubbles back into solution, and decompress slowly. This procedure is carried out in a recompression chamber, of which there are too few; for this reason, the address and telephone number of the nearest recompression chamber should be in the possession of every diving expedition. And bear in mind that the recompression chamber you have listed down might not be open and available 24 hours a day, 7 days a week. If possible, check that it will be operative if you should require it.

Symptoms of decompression sickness usually consist of pains in the joints of the limbs, itching or swelling of the skin, dizziness, shortness of breath (not necessarily all of them at once) and, in the case of spinal bends, paralysis. If the bubbles are large enough, they can cause a blockage in the heart, with obvious results.

There are two methods of avoiding the bends. The simplest—and safest—procedure is to avoid the maximum nitrogen absorption level. If a depth deeper than 10 metres is to be attempted, then no more than 1132 litres (40 cubic feet)—or half a 2000 litres (72 cubic feet) cylinder—of air should be consumed in any 12 hour period. Alternatively, if a maximum depth limit of 10 metres is imposed, then it is difficult to reach a dangerous level of nitrogen, and you could with safety use a twin-set with two 2000 litre cylinders and enjoy a long dive.

Should longer, deeper dives be contemplated, then a dangerous level of nitrogen absorption might be reached, and this excess nitrogen should, ideally, be gradually dissipated by a procedure known as decompressing. This entails ascending at a speed no faster than 18 metres (60 feet) per minute, and stopping at certain depths for regulated periods of time laid down by decompression tables. For example, if a dive to a depth of 48 metres (about 150 feet) is planned we find, by reference to the decompression tables (see Appendix A), that if we exceed a certain time at this depth—including the descent—then our ascent of 18 metres per minute will have to be interrupted, at the very least, by a five minute stop at 6 metres, and another at 3 metres. And this additional time has to be taken into consideration when estimating the required supply of air.

You will notice a 'limiting line' marked on the decompression tables. This is for second and subsequent dives within 12 hours. A diver carrying out a dive on Table 1 above the limiting line, may carry out a second and subsequent dives to depths not greater than 9 metres, without time restriction or further decompression. If, however, he is required to dive again to a depth exceeding 9 metres within 4 hours of a previous dive to 9 metres or less, or within 12 hours of a previous dive to more than 9 metres, he may do so only if he is given the stops for a combined dive. A diver who has carried out a dive below the limiting line should not dive again for at least 12 hours.

Complicated? Not really. In any case, you can make it a lot easier by adhering to the rule that you should only have one good dive a day.

One important point to note is that decompression sickness is variable. Because you inadvertently didn't decompress when you should have done, but didn't get the bends, does not mean you are immune—another time you might be struck down when just falling short of decompression requirements. Like alcohol, the bends strike when you least expect it. In fact, in a minute proportion of cases divers have been known to get the bends even after they have followed decompression procedure—there is no such thing as a 100% safe set of tables.

Nitrogen narcosis

This is another dangerous side-effect of nitrogen breathed under pressure. Although given colourful names such as 'rapture of the deep' and 'diver's alcohol' nitrogen narcosis is a possible danger to all divers working at a depth greater than 30 metres or 100 feet. The effect, as with the bends varies with different people, indeed, it varies from day to day in the same person, and the symptoms can commence at any depth from 30 metres down.

The symptoms are often similar to alcoholic intoxication; every little action becomes muddled, thinking is confused, and the instinct for self-preservation can disappear. This has resulted in divers happily swimming down to depths greater than they would normally consider—perhaps under the delusion that they were surfacing—or removing their mouthpiece, considering it no longer necessary. Little imagination is required to realize the dangers open to the diver while in this condition. The symptoms will vanish if an ascent, often of only a metre or two, is made, and there are no after-effects.

Should you realize that you have experienced a loss of judgement, perception or control while under water, make an immediate but steady ascent until the condition clears; and do not return to that depth the same day.

If your partner shows such symptoms, and in addition seems reluctant to ascend, don't attempt to force the issue —at least, not from the front. Swim round to his rear, grasp his cylinder, and fin upwards.

The important thing to remember is to be on the lookout for symptoms of nitrogen narcosis whenever you are deeper than the 30 metre mark.

Anoxia, hyperventilation and reduced breathing

One of the later symptoms of lack of oxygen (anoxia) is unconsciousness; the danger, should this happen under water and with no help nearby, is obvious.

Probably the most common cause of blackout under water among spearfishermen is hyperventilation. This is the act of breathing deeply and heavily for a minute or two, thereby reducing the proportion of carbon dioxide in the system. The reason this is done is because carbon dioxide triggers the mechanism that tells you you need to breathe (see Carbon dioxide poisoning). With some of the carbon dioxide flushed out by hyperventilation, the desire to breathe is reduced and a snorkel diver can last longer under water. The trouble with this is that it is quite easy to reach a pitch where the desire to breathe is subdued to the point that you can blackout through lack of oxygen before your body can warn you of this danger. Several swimmers and snorkel divers have died in swimming pools because they practiced hyperventilation; goodness knows how many snorkel divers and spearfishermen who never returned, or were just found drowned, did so as a result of hyperventilation. A considerable number as far as we can tell.

Make it a personal rule *never* to practice hyperventilation. A couple of deep breaths before submerging is permissible, but any more and you are courting trouble.

Anoxia can also strike the diver who tries to economize on air. Although a shallow, reduced breathing rate that verges on breath-holding can reduce the consumption of air in the cylinder, this is a dangerous way of trying to extend a dive. Reduced breathing reduces the oxygen supply in the system, and this can easily cause a blackout.

A lack of oxygen can also be brought about by a faulty or contaminated air supply.

Oxygen poisoning

The compressed air cylinders of the modern subaqua swimmer are often stated in the popular Press as containing oxygen—a dangerous mistake. This is, no doubt, based on Second World War knowledge, when frogmen used cylinders containing pure oxygen; this was continually re-breathed, the exhaled carbon dioxide being removed via an absorbent, so that no tell-tale bubbles would be given off to inform the enemy. This is called closed-circuit equipment and, although of use to the military and some specialist applications, should never be used by the club or amateur diver. And pure oxygen should *never* be used in aqualung cylinders, for the following reasons:

Pure oxygen, when breathed for too long a period, has marked harmful effects. Breathed under a pressure of two atmospheres or more—a depth of 10 metres (33 feet), or deeper—you can suffer oxygen poisoning almost immediately. The symptoms include coughing, vomiting, convulsions and unconsciousness; thus the reason for most clubs banning oxygen diving are obvious.

Oxygen poisoning can also affect the subaqua diver using compressed air; at a depth of around 90 metres or 300 feet, the amount of oxygen in the compressed air supply would approximate the proportion of two atmospheres, with the obvious danger of oxygen poisoning. But as the amateur diver should not even contemplate depths in this region, the problem should not arise.

Carbon monoxide poisoning

Carbon monoxide is a colourless, odorless gas, poisonous when inhaled, that is formed by the incomplete oxidation of carbon—exhaust fumes being the most common. Carbon monoxide will contaminate the air supply if the exhaust outlet of a petrol-driven compressor is too close to the air intake; or if other exhaust fumes are present, such as in a garage; or if the particular oil used in the compressor has reached a flashing point.

As with other gases, the detrimental effects of carbon monoxide on the body will increase with quantity—and a compressed gas has more quantity. A small percentage of this gas in the breathing air can cause sickness and headache, and a large percentage can bring on unconsciousness and death. Any time an aqualung diver experiences drowsiness, giddiness, palpitations or nausea, carbon monoxide poisoning should be suspected. The face of the victim will be flushed, and he will have a rapid or irregular pulse. The treatment is plenty of fresh air—and artificial respiration if breathing has stopped.

Carbon dioxide poisoning

Normal atmospheric air contains less than 0·4 per cent carbon dioxide; after exhalation, this will increase to over 4 per cent. If the breath is held, this increased percentage of carbon dioxide will build up and, as this gas has a direct effect on respiration, will stimulate the desire to breathe.

When the *inhaled* air contains more than 2 per cent carbon dioxide—at atmospheric pressure—breathlessness will occur. A further increase will cause heavy panting, headache, and exhaustion. At a 10 per cent concentration, unconsciousness and death are not very far away. This is one of the reasons why an aqualung diver will become breathless after comparatively little exertion under water, for, at 20 metres or 66 feet, three times the normal amount of carbon dioxide is being inhaled, and this renders the diver more prone to fatigue.

4

Essential Equipment

The equipment described here is the very basic apparatus needed to transform the snorkel diver or skin-diver, who uses only fins, mask and perhaps snorkel, into an aqualung diver capable of staying under water for comparatively long periods. The average non-diver has a hazy, roughly accurate grasp of how the modern aqualung diver breathes under

Regulator air flow requirements		
Water surface	Normal consumption 1 ft³/min	Exertion consumption 3 ft³/min
10 m 33 ft	2 ft³/min	6 ft³/min
20 m 66 ft	3 ft³/min	9 ft³/min
30 m 99 ft	4 ft³/min	12 ft³/min

This shows just how much extra air the diver breathes to compensate for ambient pressure. Thus at a depth of 30 metres he will have four times the surface requirement in his lungs. This, however, only takes up the same space that it does on the surface because it is compressed.   (*US Divers*)

water; he sucks on a mouthpiece, drawing air through the tube or tubes attached to the cylinder of compressed air strapped on his back. What is not so apparent is the mechanism that intercepts the tube(s) before it arrives at the cylinder. This is known as a regulator or demand valve, and it adjusts the flow of air, as the diver inhales, to the correct quantity and pressure.

Principles and selection of the regulator

The operation of the original regulator is simplicity itself, and although there have been innovations, the principles remain the same.

Basically, the nerve centre is a rubber diaphragm, one side of which is in contact with the water, and the other with the air from the cylinder. The weight of water creates a pressure on the external side, causing it to bulge inwards; this bulge actuates a lever, releasing air from the cylinder into the space contained by the internal side of the diaphragm. As the air released reaches the same pressure as the external water the bulge is pressed back, easing the pressure on the actuating lever and stopping the flow of air. It is this principle that allows the aqualung diver to draw air, because his inhalation, creating a partial vacuum and reducing the pressure on the internal side of the diaphragm, causes the accompanying inward bulge that actuates the air release lever.

The above principle—a lever, actuating air direct from a cylinder or chamber, is called a stage, and a regulator operating solely by this mechanism is called a single-stage. This is the most basic type of regulator; working parts are minimal and the regulator, with a little knowledge, is relatively easy to service and repair. Early single-stage mechanisms suffered because they required a relatively strong 'suck' on the mouthpiece to start the flow of air, and tended to pull heavy when low on air. However, innovations such as longer or articulated levers, and more precise construction, have almost eliminated these disadvantages.

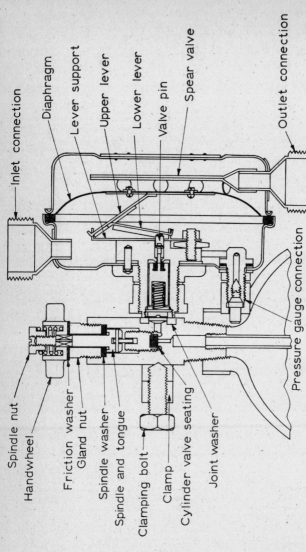

Inlet connection

Diaphragm

Lever support

Upper lever

Lower lever

Valve pin

Spear valve

Outlet connection

Spindle nut

Handwheel

Friction washer

Gland nut

Spindle washer

Spindle and tongue

Clamping bolt

Clamp

Cylinder valve seating

Joint washer

Pressure gauge connection

Cut-through diagram of the Siebe Gorman 'Mistral' single stage twin hose regulator. Also a cut-away view of a cylinder valve.

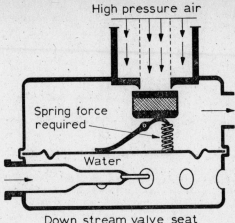

High pressure air

Spring force required

Water

Down stream valve seat

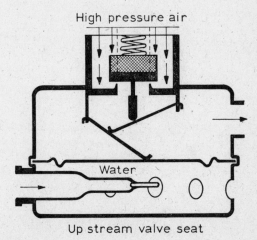

High pressure air

Water

Up stream valve seat

Outline of a typical single stage twin hose regulator. (*US Divers*)

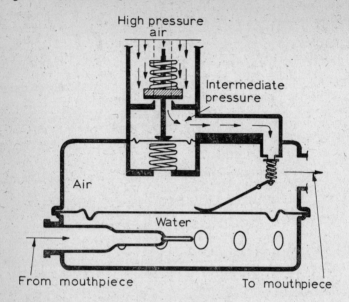

High pressure
air

Intermediate
pressure

Air

Water

From mouthpiece

To mouthpiece

Outline of a two stage twin hose regulator.　　　　(*US Divers*)

Although the single-stage regulator is perfectly adequate for most purposes, some divers—particularly professionals—require a regulator that has a minimum of breathing resistance, and one that can use the last breath of air in the cylinder. This is achieved by the introduction of another 'stage', which takes the form of a reducing valve (operating on the same principle as the first stage) fitting between the cylinder and the final demand chamber. Its purpose is to reduce the cylinder air pressure before it passes into the demand chamber, ensuring a smoother flow of air. This type is called a two-stage regulator, and although it is capable of better performances when the diver is breathing hard while working under water, it is more complicated and more difficult to service and repair than its single-stage brother.

The original regulator was a twin-hose type. This has two corrugated rubber tubes, one tube carrying air from the regulator to the mouthpiece and the other conveying the exhaled air from the mouthpiece back to the rear of the regulator, where it is released into the water.

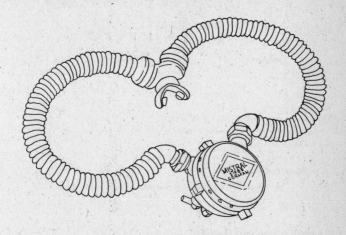

A typical twin hose regulator.

Another, and currently more popular type, is the single hose, or split-stage regulator, which is of two-stage construction. The first stage is fitted at the cylinder head; a small bore tube leads off from here to the mouthpiece, where the second stage is located. The exhaled air is released via two metal or plastic tubes attached to the mouthpiece. Some divers do not like the heavy mouthpiece of the single hose regulator, nor the fact that exhaled air is released around the face, which can obscure vision when you are looking up; but this type was originally cheaper to produce, and it does make a neater parcel when trying to fit your gear into a suitcase.

There are, then, three types of regulator generally available, and their respective merits are shown in the

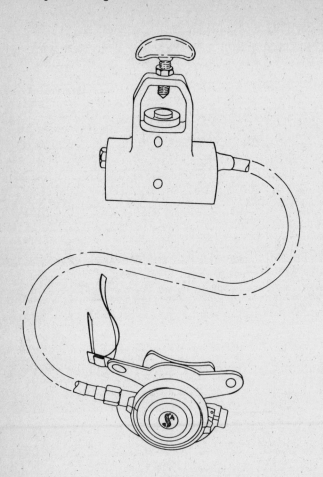

Single hose regulators usually have two stages, one clamped to the
pillar valve of the cylinder, and the other attached to the mouthpiece. The item above shows the first stage of a Scubapro
regulator—this one has a sonic device that warns the diver when
his air is low—the lower item is the mouthpiece and second stage.

table. Examine the table carefully before you consider what type to buy. Pay particular attention to the fact that single hose regulators tend to obscure vision when you look upwards, because the exhaust air is released around the face and the bubbles drift past your eyes when your chin is lifted. This is no great problem for the average diver, but if you want to take photographs under water, you will lose some of those interesting silhouette shots of divers and fish

Regulator Table

Type	Advantages	Disadvantages
Twin hose single-stage	Relatively cheap. Easy to maintain and repair.	Tends to pull hard when cylinder pressure is low or when diver is breathing heavily. The corrugated air hoses can be punctured.
Twin hose two-stage	Easy air flow, even when cylinder pressure is low and when breathing heavily. Exhaled air is released behind you.	The most expensive type of demand valve. Difficult to repair. The corrugated air hoses can be punctured.
Single hose two-stage	Cheapest type of demand valve. More compact than twin hose models. The air hose is almost impossible to puncture.	Mouthpiece is heavy. Exhaled air is released around the face, making it of less value for underwater photography.

framed against the surface light, while waiting for the bubbles to clear.

It is obviously important for the diver to be able to tell when the air in his cylinder is low. There are two mechanisms which can perform this function, the pressure gauge and the air reserve system. The former is attached to the demand valve or manifold via a high-pressure hose; a needle on the face of the pressure gauge indicates the pressure (or amount of) air available at any stage of the dive. In the air reserve system, the air becomes very hard to draw when the pressure is low, and a reserve lever has to be pulled to obtain the remaining air, thus warning the diver that it is time to ascend.

Although the air reserve method may seem to possess the prime advantage because it physically informs the diver that he is low on air—he may be too absorbed to look at his gauge—in practice this does not work out; with experience, a diver will automatically keep a constant check on his gauge. Furthermore, a gauge actually performs three functions: it will inform you when you are low on air; of the amount of air available throughout the dive; and of the amount of air in the cylinder before you dive. If the last-named should seem unimportant, it should be pointed

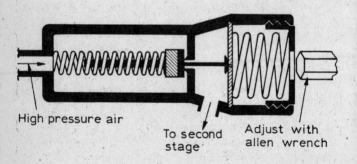

High pressure air

To second stage

Adjust with allen wrench

A fairly typical first stage of a single hose regulator.   (*US Divers*)

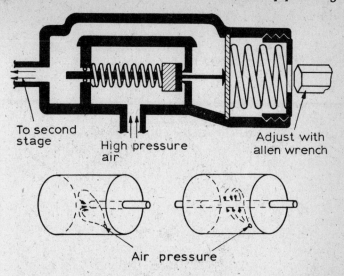

To second stage

High pressure air

Adjust with allen wrench

Air pressure

If a single hose regulator has a balanced first stage it has a better performance. This illustration shows the principle.   (*US Divers*)

out that errors can occur when compressor crews are busy at the height of the season, and cylinders can be returned only half full, or almost empty, by mistake. The pressure gauge allows you to check this instantly, an air reserve won't. And bobbing in a boat several miles out at sea is not the time to find out. Remember, a gauge gives you an instant check that your cylinder(s) is fully charged; an air reserve will only operate when the air is dangerously low.

Regulators need regular and proper maintenance. After each dive, thoroughly rinse the regulator and hose(s) in fresh water, holding a finger over the filter at the back to ensure that water does not enter at this point. Store it away from excessive heat, and from sharp objects that might cut or puncture a hose. A regulator should not be fastened to a cylinder until just before a dive, and it should be removed as soon as possible afterwards; if left on a cylinder, it is more liable to damage. Working parts wear, and rubber perishes, so ensure that your regulator is overhauled *every* winter, even if apparently in perfect working order.

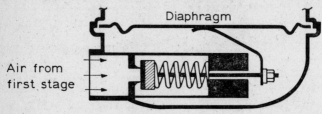

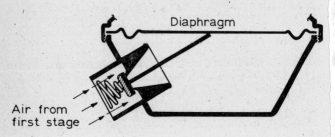

The second or mouthpiece stage of a single hose regulator can have a piston valve (above) or a tilt valve (below). There are definite, positive advantages in the piston mechanism, but the tilt valve is more inexpensive to make.　　(*US Divers*)

Cylinders

Cylinders provide the means of housing the compressed *air* (not oxygen) in a portable form enabling the diver to exist under water for indefinite periods. Manufactured from steel alloy or aluminium alloy, cylinders (also known as 'tanks' or 'bottles') come in a variety of sizes, and virtually every country lays down a set of manufacturing specifications for aqualung cylinders; in Britain for instance, it is the Home Office, and in the USA it is the Interstate Commerce Commission (ICC). Each authority imposes slightly different specifications, and while in general they all seem to work perfectly well, it is best to use the cylinders approved for a specific country in that country, for example a Home Office approved cylinder when diving around Britain. The reason I suggest this—and I admit it's only my own opinion—it because if there should be an accident or incident your insurance position might become difficult if the above conditions don't apply.

The storage capacity of an aqualung cylinder is quoted in cubic feet (cu. ft.), or litres; thus a cylinder quoted as having a capacity of, say, 40 cu. ft. would contain this amount of air, in compressed form, when filled to the appropriate pressure marked on the neck or collar of the cylinder (and *every* cylinder should be so marked). This last point is very important, because cylinders have a maximum pressure that they can safely hold. For instance, given two cylinders of identical dimensions, one having a maximum pressure of 120 atmospheres and the other of 240 atmospheres, the latter will contain twice the amount of air than the former when both are correctly charged or filled.

With the world-wide change to metrication, the measuring of cylinder capacity and pressures has become extremely involved. For instance a cylinder can be rated as having an air capacity of 70 cu. ft., or 1981 litres, or 1·981 cubic metres; and the same cylinder could have a maximum working pressure of 2250 psi, 120 atmospheres, or 123 bars! All virtually the same, all virtually confusing. And I'm afraid I can't help you out with an easy formula: for the next few years you are going to find one manufacturer talking in cu. ft. and another talking in litres or cubic metres—and at the same time most countries are at different stages of conversion to metric measurements or S.I. units. For this reason I have included two tables giving equivalents

c

for cylinder capacity and pressure. I suggest you use a unit from each (litres, and ats or bars) and convert when necessary.

Aqualung cylinders should be handled with extreme care, because the pressures involved make them potentially as dangerous as bombs. Rough handling is not the only factor that could cause a cylinder to explode; poor maintenance could cause the interior walls of a steel cylinder to rust, reducing the thickness and with it the margin of safety. Cylinders charged to pressures higher than those stamped can suffer from fatigue. Remember, an exploding cylinder would almost certainly kill everyone nearby, so it pays to take care.

There is an internationally recognized colour code for gases stored in cylinders, to avoid the possibility of a cylinder being charged with an unrequired gas. That for breathing air is grey, with black and white quartering round the neck and shoulder of the valve end. Unfortunately, this code has been largely ignored by the cylinder manufacturers, who produce cylinder colours in orange, yellow, blue—you name it. Tests have proved that the best colour combination under water is that of black and white, the same as the quartering recommended for breathing air cylinders; but still cylinders of odd colours are sold. I suspect that this problem is more the result of interference by the marketing and sales boys than for any reasons of safety. Still, the practice is pretty widespread, and in some parts of the world it is impossible to obtain grey cylinders with black and white quartering. It does not cause any general problem, because I have never known a compressor operator refuse to charge air because the cylinder was a non-code colour. Perhaps I'm being fussy.

Regulations also exist for the testing of cylinders, and again they vary from country to country: for example the Home Office suggests every two years. But most organizations involved with diving recommend testing two years after purchase, and every year thereafter.

A cylinder should never be stored with the valve tap open, because the compressor fills the cylinder with comparatively dry air, and if the tap is left open moisture-laden air would enter.

A dented, deeply cut or abraded cylinder should be relegated to the scrap-heap.

Approximate Comparisons

Cylinder Capacity	
Cubic feet	Litres
40	1132
50	1415
60	1698
70	1980
75	2123
80	2264

Cylinder Pressure	
psi	ats or bars
1800	121
2000	136
2250	151
2500	166
2650	177
3000	202

The harness

The harness should be selected as much for its comfort of fit as for its practical use. Aqualung equipment often has to be carried a considerable distance on foot in order to reach some diving sites, and an unbalanced, uncomfortable harness will chafe and exhaust its owner.

Although three (and even four) cylinders are sometimes worn by professionals and experimental groups, the single- and two-cylinder harnesses are the most popular among amateur divers. Should you contemplate an aqualung unit of two cylinders, then have a look at the several harnesses on the market that are convertible, fitting either one or two cylinders. You won't always require two cylinders, and a long walk carrying a heavy, bulky twin-set is rather pointless if a short dive in shallow water is contemplated. And a single is much more convenient for winter training in the pool.

Apart from holding your cylinder(s) in place securely and comfortably, a good harness should possess efficient quick-release buckles and be easy to take off while under water, or when swimming on the surface; for if you ever need to jettison your aqualung, you will probably be in a hurry, tired, and exhausted—and in this condition you don't want to have to fumble around, or indulge in energetic contortions.

The air supply

Too many aqualung divers are vague about the contents of their cylinders. A compressor should supply medically pure—or very nearly so—air, and although air supplied by the majority of commercial and club compressors comes up to this standard, it is a fact that occasionally, owing perhaps to poor siting or bad maintenance, air of dubious quality is supplied. Contamination can occur in several ways: exhaust fumes from cars (many compressors are in garages) for example, can result in the induction of dangerous carbon monoxide; or moisture—laden air, the result of an inadequate drying filter, can cause water to form in the cylinder; if a cylinder is filled quickly, heated air is forced into the cylinder, and this can cause condensation on the inside walls. Oil and dust can be particularly harmful to the lungs, and both can be introduced into the air supply by an inefficient compressor.

The air endurance of a given cylinder is variable. This is not the fault of the equipment, but rather that of the user. It is generally assumed that the average person uses one cubic foot ($28 \cdot 3$ litres) of air per minute on land, and this seems to give us a good basis for calculations: a 40 cu. ft. (1132 litre) cylinder would suffice a diver for 40 minutes at the surface; at 33 feet (10 metres)—double the pressure—the air would last for 20 minutes at 99 feet (30 metres)—double again—it would be 10 minutes, and so on. However this rule, in practice, is at best only a very

rough guide, because various human factors have to be taken into consideration. A novice diver uses air at a much faster rate than an experienced diver, and even the latter's varies from day to day. Then again, a diver lazily browsing around will show an apparent economy of air against his partner who is working furiously, in exactly the same way that a man walking uses less air than one who is running— it's just that you notice these things more when your air supply is limited. Also, the average diver does not stay at the same depth and the calculations involved e.g. 5 minutes at 25 feet, 7 minutes at 31 feet etc., would necessitate the use of a computer even if humans were not variable.

It is only logical that the aqualung diver should attempt to obtain the maximum underwater time from his air supply; but to this end it is dangerous to practice breath-holding. Not only is this foolhardy, it does not extend the air supply. Minimum air consumption is the result of a lazy, steady breathing rhythm; try to avoid exertion and, if swimming against a current over a rocky or seaweed bed, crawl along the bottom, pulling yourself along hand-over-hand. When swimming with the current, use your fins just enough to keep suspended, letting the water carry you along. But make sure you don't overdo the latter—you can drift a long way from the boat or base without even realizing it.

5

Additional Equipment

The only really essential items of equipment for the scuba swimmer are: mask, fins, regulator, cylinder and harness. But in practice there are other articles that, while not absolutely essential for underwater swimming, are almost as important if the diver is to have a safe, comfortable dive. Only the foolhardy or ignorant would omit a snorkel tube from their basic equipment; it could be a life-saver if you surfaced out of air and with a long swim to the nearest landing point. For similar reasons, the lifejacket should be worn on every dive. And although protective clothing or diving suits are of great importance in cold waters such as those that surround the British Isles and the northernmost coasts of America, even in the sunny Mediterranean the diver requires some form of protective insulation if diving at even a moderate depth for a considerable length of time.

Principles and selection of protective clothing

The cold hazard
Cooling of the temperature of the body—hypothermia—is a serious hazard in diving; even at sites where the water is generally warm for ordinary swimmers or shallow diving, it is often quite cold deep down, creating a problem for the diver venturing beyond average depths. In cold water there is a loss of body heat which is absorbed by the water,

and this loss increases with decreasing water temperatures.

The effects of a loss of body heat are considerable. As the body temperature is lowered, the extremities cool first, the internal organs within the torso being the last to cool. This is the result of the body preserving essential warmth for the vital parts. However, this protective mechanism is not so effective at the head, which is in effect an extremity, and the spinal cord, which is near the surface of the body.

With hypothermia, one of the symptoms is the onset of mental confusion, which often means that the diver becomes unaware of his condition. The first symptom, common to all of us, is shivering, which occurs in a body as a means of producing heat. When this mechanism is no longer effective, the temperature of the internal organs starts to drop and reflexes and movement are impaired, with the diver becoming progressively incapable of adequate thought, judgement, and the performance of simple physical actions. The final symptoms can include abnormal vision, and will certainly result in unconsciousness and collapse—usually with fatal results.

Without protective clothing, the diver's capacity to resist cold depends mainly on the layer of fat under his skin. It is a fact that fat people survive cold better than thin people. Unfortunately, unless the layer of fat is developed as a result of constant contact with cold conditions (this happens with long distance swimmers), it is usually indicative of a lack of fitness—and any diver should avoid this.

Although the diver cannot entirely eliminate the problem of cold water exposure, he can, with protective clothing, minimize it. For instance, in water at a temperature of 50°F or 10°C, an unclothed swimmer would last about $3\frac{1}{2}$ hours before succumbing to exposure. In the same conditions, but clothed with a wet suit of $\frac{3}{16}$ inch (4·8mm) thick material, the same swimmer could be expected to survive for 24 hours. This illustrates the effectiveness of protective clothing. Even a garment such as an ordinary

sweater would to a certain extent reduce the flow of water next to the skin, and as a result slow down the loss of body heat, enabling the diver or swimmer to survive longer.

Wet suits

As the name indicates, wet suits are not watertight. The principle is simple: The suit consists of a material—usually a foam rubber or synthetic rubber—that is close fitting. Water seeps in and is trapped between the skin and the inner layer of the suit; the body warms this thin film of water and the suit material acts as an insulator, retaining the warmth (or, rather, reducing the heat loss) to a remarkable degree.

There is a definite relation between the thickness of the wet suit material and the effectiveness of the insulation. A thick material will retain warmth much better than a thin material; but this is not the only criterion in the selection of a suit for diving. A very thick (say $1\frac{3}{32}$ inch or 10·3mm) material, while providing for maximum heat retention will, to a certain extent, hinder the movement of the diver. This will not matter so much to the diver who is constantly diving in water that is around freezing point, but the diver who usually swims in warmer waters will find a thinner material of around $\frac{3}{16}$ inch or 4·8mm perfectly adequate and much more comfortable.

The first wet suit materials were made of foam rubber. The foam structure consists of millions of tiny air cells, and these cells assist the insulating properties of the material. Nowadays, although the foam structure has been kept, the rubber has been replaced by neoprene. This is because rubber is a very perishable product, while neoprene is remarkably resistant to the effects of sunlight, heat and most chemicals.

The principal disadvantage of foam materials is their loss of buoyancy under pressure. The fact that the air or gas cells render the material positively buoyant at surface level invariably means that the diver has to weight himself

in order to be able to descend. As he descends, the minute cells in the material are compressed by the pressure of water, and lose buoyancy. This means that a diver correctly weighted at the surface becomes increasingly over-weighted at depth. Returning to the surface then becomes more of an effort than descending. In an emergency this negative buoyancy at depth could seriously hinder a diver if he has to surface quickly. It is for this reason that the weights a diver carries are usually provided with some means of jettisoning them quickly.

Another disadvantage of this effect of compression with depth is that the suit material actually reduces in thickness and provides less insulation. A diver will feel the cold increasing in intensity as he goes deeper, even if the water remains at the same temperature, because the suit material's ability to retain or conserve heat has been reduced.

Despite these considerable disadvantages, the wet suit is the most popular type of protective clothing, and is used by more than 95% of amateur divers. There are several reasons for this. The wet suit is very convenient for the amateur diver; it requires no special waterproofing seals, no undergarments, and if torn might become uncomfortable but never dangerous. It is also infinitely easier to get into—and out of—than the cumbersome dry suit, which frequently requires the assistance of a second person.

The wet suit should be a snug yet comfortable fit. Wet suits can be purchased ready-made in various sizes— and prices—or in the form of a do-it-yourself kit; the sheets of neoprene are supplied along with patterns. The patterns are marked out on the sheets and the neoprene cut to the marks. The 'stitching' is achieved by means of contact neoprene adhesive and butted (joined edge-to-edge) seams. This forms a secure bond that requires little maintenance. These kits provide the best value for money if you can afford the time. They have the added advantage if the final fit does not quite fit e.g. it's baggy at the knees, then you would be quite happy to snip a little material out of each knee and

re-join. But if you've paid a lot of money for a ready-made model you'd be less keen—and probably end up with baggy knees!

A nylon lining bonded to the surface—inside or outside, usually the former—is no longer an innovation and most diving suits are nylon lined. This provides great strength and makes the material virtually tear proof. Although a torn wet suit is no danger to the diver, the exposed portion of anatomy will make that area a little uncomfortable in very cold water.

Wet suits are of fairly uniform design, but variations do occur, particularly in the jacket. This can have the hood attached, or separate. And the system of fastening the front will be by heavy duty zip or a Velcro-type fastener. The pullover-type jacket has no front opening at all, which, although slightly warmer, is almost impossible to get off without help. The type of jacket ultimately selected is a matter of personal choice.

Dry suits

The principle of the dry suit is virtually the opposite of the wet suit. The suit is (or should be) watertight, and warm clothing is worn underneath it.

It is a comparatively loose-fitting garment (to allow for undergarments) composed, usually, of sheet rubber or neoprene, sometimes reinforced with fabric. Tight-fitting waterproof seals are incorporated at the wrists and neck and, in a two-piece suit, some form of sealing, usually a cummerbund, at the waist. Undergarments are worn because sheet rubber is a poor insulator and some form of reducing heat loss is necessary.

When the diver is dressed, the undergarments will retain some air in them, and it is necessary to vent off as much of this as possible—otherwise buoyancy will be affected at depth in much the same way as with wet suits. Venting is a simple procedure and consists of inserting one finger under the wrist seal of the opposite wrist and sub-

water is a corroding agent at the best of times and all suits, after a dive, should be thoroughly rinsed in fresh water and dried. Don't put a suit away unless it has been dried properly; even fresh water will accelerate deterioration if the material is stored damp.

When the suit is thoroughly dry, check it over and repair any tears, or reinforce any abrasions, dust it carefully with french chalk or non-perfumed talcum and fold carefully. It should be stored in a dry place away from excessive heat or sharp implements.

If a suit has any oil on it, wash this off with a detergent. If you haven't got detergent, spirit will do at a pinch, but remember that such solvents can remove the adhesive on seams and joins.

Particular attention should be given to the wrist and neck seals of dry suits. These are generally of pure rubber and perish easily.

Pre-dive preparation

Protective clothing is only one of the requirements for a warm, comfortable dive. If you are cold when you enter the water, some of the effectiveness of the suit is lost.

Ensure that you are comfortably warm before you get into your suit. If your body is chilled before a dive, no amount of protective clothing will warm you. This applies particularly to the extremities—hands and feet. If you are wearing a wet suit, it is often useful to pour warm water into it, via neck and wrists, to minimize the entry of cold water and pre-warm your body.

There are other considerations. For instance, aspirin has the effect of lowering body temperature to a certain extent; and an excess of alcohol in the blood will seriously impair the body's ability to generate heat.

After-dive procedure

You don't want to have a good dive and then get so

thoroughly chilled afterwards that you go down with a cold or something more serious. So plan your post-dive procedure carefully.

The most common reason for chilling after a dive is because of the effect of evaporation chill when you take your wet suit off. If possible, undress in a warm place and have a large towel and warm clothes ready.

If you do get severely chilled, the best remedy is a hot bath. In fact, a hot bath has even been known to have revived people who have apparently died of hypothermia. The bath should be as hot as you can bear testing it with your hand.

Weight belt

The positive buoyancy of protective clothing is such that some form of weighting or ballast is required if the diver is to be able to submerge at all. The usual method of doing this is to wear a belt to which lead weights are attached. The point to remember here is that it is impossible (unless you have an ABLJ, which is described later) to be correctly weighted at all depths. This is because the compression on the suit material (see previous section, Wet Suits) reduces the buoyancy of the material with depth, and of course the weights become proportionately 'heavier'. In practice, the diver soon gets used to being slightly heavy at depth.

The best way to weight yourself is so that you can float comfortably on the surface when fully equipped. This means that it is a little harder to swim down the first ten feet (3m) or so, but this is worth it for the extra safety on the surface. It is on the surface where most of the diving incidents occur.

The function of a weight belt is to assist the diver to descend. It follows that should he wish to dispense with this facility to help him ascend in an emergency, he will want to do it easily and quickly. So a weight belt **must** possess a quick-release that is reliable. An ordinary belt strung with lumps of lead is a potentially lethal piece of equipment. Anybody wishing to reach a ripe old age should buy a belt that can be released with a single sharp tug. Make sure that the quick release mechanism is large and easy to find. A short length of flimsy tape actuating an otherwise excellent quick release is of little use to a diver with frozen fingers and thick, bulky gloves.

Practise releasing the weight belt (but not in a swimming pool, it might crack a tile). After the release, hold the belt away at arm's length before letting go. There is a good reason for this. A belt released and allowed to drop freely could become snagged in another item of equipment—such as a knife strapped to the leg—and an emergency is not the time to have to fumble around.

Also, the weights should be easy to attach and remove, otherwise there is a tendency to leave excessive weight on 'until the next time'. This could well mean that there will never be a next time! Why should it be necessary to remove weights once attached? Well, first of all there is a difference in density between salt and fresh water. In other words, it is easier to float in salt water, so if you weight yourself for sea diving, you will have to remove a couple of weights when diving in a lake or river—or vice versa. Or it might be something simpler like weighting for a dive in cold water, followed at a later date by a dive in warmer water when you might not wear trousers and gloves, necessitating less weights.

Lifejackets

There are three types of lifejacket in general use by divers throughout the world, the BC (buoyancy compensator) the SLJ (surface lifejacket) and the ABLJ (adjustable buoyancy lifejacket).

The BC is commonly used in the South Pacific area, and is not a lifejacket in the true sense of the term. It is in fact a waterproof bag or jacket—of the same general shape as most lifejackets—with the only opening at the bottom of the bag. A long rubber tube is fixed to this opening, and the extreme end of the tube has a closure, such as a simple plug, over the end. The principle is as follows: before the dive the diver unseals or unplugs the end of the tube and sucks all the air out of the jacket, replacing the plug. As the diver descends and his suit loses buoyancy, he can unplug the tube again and blow a few puffs of air into the jacket to retain neutral buoyancy. It is a simple yet effective method of achieving neutral buoyancy underwater, but it is of no use whatsoever if, for example, a diver's regulator fails at depth, because there is then no means of inflating the jacket. And it is worth noting that most ABLJs can be used as buoyancy compensators, yet also have the ability to inflate the jacket fully, irrespective of the diver's air supply.

The SLJ, as the name implies, is designed for surface buoyancy only. It is inflated by means of a gas cartridge of the type used for filling soda syphons (the gas is a non-breathable variety, usually CO_2). This cartridge only contains sufficient gas to fill the jacket fully while on the surface of the water, because it is designed for sailors, who only require surface support. However, for divers this design or principle creates problems. For example, if the jacket is inflated fully at a depth of 10 metres, its volume, and buoyancy, will be roughly halved, and at 30 metres the volume and buoyancy will be about one quarter of that at the surface. In practical terms this means that an SLJ that has a buoyancy of 5 kilos on the surface will only have a lifting capacity of about 1·5 kilos at 30 metres. Now there is no doubt that a buoyancy of 1·5 kilos is better than nothing, but there is another factor to take into account. At this depth the diver's suit, if he is wearing one, will also have only one quarter of its surface buoyancy. So in practice the average diver may well have no buoyancy with a fully inflated SLJ at 30 metres unless he drops his weight belt. And in some cases e.g., if his cylinders are heavy, the rest of his equipment might anchor him to the bottom regardless.

It is obvious, then, that the SLJ, while ideal for 'surface' watersports (sailing, surfing etc.) is far from ideal for the diver. However, it is better than nothing. The SLJ was, for many years, the only lifejacket available for the diver, and as such has proved a valuable if imperfect item of equipment. It still is where cash is the prime consideration, and in this case the expression 'your money or your life' often has real meaning.

The ABLJ was developed to fill the need for a lifejacket that could develop full buoyancy at any depth down to about 50 metres or more. To do this, particular problems of design and function had to be overcome. To obtain full buoyancy at depth the ABLJ has to have a cylinder of gas with a larger capacity than the SLJ soda-syphon variety. This has been achieved by fitting the ABLJ with a cylinder that could be re-filled from a standard aqualung cylinder; and this method has the additional advantage of providing the diver with a separate source of breathing air for emergencies. Virtually every ABLJ utilizes the principle of a separate cylinder of compressed air for inflation purposes. There are a few types that inflate the lifejacket directly from the aqualung cylinder—usually by means of a hose connection extended from the pressure gauge.

Another problem in designing an ABLJ is the fact that air compressed at depth expands as it rises to the surface. This means that a lifejacket inflated fully at depth would be ruptured by the expanding air on ascent. So all ABLJs are fitted with a pressure relief valve to allow the excess air to vent off as the diver ascends.

Having been designed for divers, the ABLJ would seem to be the best lifejacket for all divers, but unfortunately it is not that simple. There are other problems, and these are caused by that most variable and unreliable piece of diving equipment—the diver.

Because the ABLJ will jet a diver from some 20 metres to the surface in something like 15 seconds there are the obvious dangers of embolism and/or decompression sick-

ness. For untrained novices, the main danger of using an
ABLJ is embolism in all its forms. To use an ABLJ a diver
should be well trained and experienced—both in general
diving and use of the ABLJ. In many clubs they will only
let new members use a SLJ until the diving officer con-
siders they have enough experience to use an ABLJ with
safety. Some clubs even have training courses in ABLJ use,
and this is the ideal. Limiting beginners to a SLJ has the
obvious merit that beginners are not allowed to go very
deep anyway, and so have less need of an ABLJ than an
experienced diver, who will probably be diving to greater
depths.

Selecting an ABLJ

There is widespread agreement that the ABLJ, which has
the merit of being able to bring a diver back to the surface
from depths as deep as 50 metres, is the best lifejacket for
the experienced diver, even though there are some dangers
in the rapid ascent.

This being so, what are the features to look for, and are
there any other problems? Well, there are several, but the
main one is—once you're on the way up, can you stop, or
slow down? After all, you might be surfacing under the
diving boat, so you'll want to be able to control the ascent
sometimes.

All ABLJs are fitted with relief valves for releasing the
excess air that expands on ascent. Some valves are an
integral part of the breathing hoses which are often provided for utilizing the jacket's supply of air in an emergency,
or for oral inflation, while some valves are a separate unit.
A method of bleeding off additional air is usually provided
so that an ascending diver (having closed the inflation
cylinder) can slow down or, by venting off completely,
stop. This is a very important facility because you never
know what you might be surfacing under, particularly in
water of low visibility. This additional bleed-off is achieved
by different means in various jackets—and the amount of

bleed-off obtained varies widely. With some jackets it is not possible to do more than slow down your ascent, while others enable you to come to a complete halt within several metres. The ability to be able to do this is an important safety factor to consider.

The capacity of the inflation cylinder is an extremely important factor, and cylinder capacities vary with different models or types. The more air a cylinder contains, the greater will be the depth from which it can haul you up. Most of the ABLJs available at the time of writing will bring a diver up from a depth of around 50 metres, so this is no problem—but we still have the problem of the diver! Life-jackets, as the name implies, are for emergencies and should only be used for such (this only applies to the cylinder). But some divers fall into the habit of continually bleeding a little air into the jacket at depth to provide a condition of neutral buoyancy. This might make a more comfortable dive, but it is at the expense of the safety margin. There is no way of checking the contents of the emergency cylinder while on a dive, and you might well be nearing the end of a dive, run into trouble, and have insufficient air for full inflation. If you want to adjust buoyancy on a dive, make sure you inflate orally through the mouthpiece—never use the cylinder. To illustrate the dangers of cylinder use; most cylinders have the capacity to lift a diver from around 50 metres. If you use up half your air, your maximum is 25 metres. Halve it again and it's only about 12 metres. And it only takes a few turns of the tap or wheel to reach this stage. Remember, lifejackets are for emergencies; don't waste valuable lifting power for the sake of convenience. (This does not necessarily apply to ABLJs that are inflated direct from the aqualung cylinder).

Every ABLJ currently on the market will bring a diver up from a depth of around 50 metres, but they don't all inflate fully at that depth. In fact, the depth of maximum inflation depends on the contents of the inflation cylinder. For those of us who can't be bothered with mathematical computations, there is a reasonably accurate way of assessing the maximum depth at which a particular model will inflate fully, and that is to see how many times the cylinder will inflate the jacket on the surface. The average will be 4–5 times. Each time the jacket is inflated, calculate it as 10 metres of depth. So the 4-inflations jacket will inflate fully at a depth of 40 metres, and the 5-inflations at 50 metres.

As mentioned, there are really two types of ABLJ. The most common uses a separate cylinder for inflation and the other uses a direct feed from the aqualung cylinder—usually via the contents gauge hose. For convenience let's call the first a *cylinder ABLJ* and the other a *direct feed ABLJ*.

The *cylinder ABLJ* has the advantage of being a separate unit that functions independently of the scuba or aqualung unit and is perfectly adequate for most diving provided you realize the potential disadvantages, which are more human than mechanical. Get into the habit of filling your cylinder before every dive. It doesn't matter if you know it's full— try it again. None of us are perfect, and I well remember a dive many years ago when I didn't bother to check my ABLJ cylinder; there was no need to, you see, I *knew* it was full. At the end of the dive I opened the tap to help me carry home a fair sized anchor I had found—and it was empty!

Take a good look at the charging clamp. This is an adaptor that couples the aqualung cylinder with the ABLJ cylinder. Some jackets have a charging clamp that is an integral part of the jacket, but some have a separate clamp. The only problem with the latter is that it can get lost. And if it is mislaid, there is always the temptation to take a chance and dive regardless.

Regarding cylinder care, this piece of equipment is usually charged and emptied far too fast to avoid condensation—which means moisture in the cylinder. Admittedly, the cylinders being smaller than aqualung cylinders the walls are proportionately thicker, but it will pay to attend to this point and get the cylinder interior checked regularly.

If the cylinder valve has parallel threads, 'O' ring sealed, you can do this yourself.

Briefly, the disadvantages of the cylinder ABLJ are:

(*a*) There is no means of checking the contents when used underwater as a buoyancy adjuster. You might forget to charge the cylinder—you'll never know until you need it!

(*b*) You can lose the charging clamp (this does not apply to all models).

(*c*) The cylinder requires frequent checks (apart from the condensation problem, if a cylinder is emptied and the jacket has some water in it, this can seep into some cylinders).

(*d*) There is a definite limit to the depth from which the jacket will bring you up; but this is a technicality which should not apply to the amateur diver.

*Direct feed ABLJ*s have the advantage of virtually un-limited air. You have a check on the amount available by means of your pressure gauge. If you have no pressure gauge, but an emergency reserve valve, then this acts as a warning device. With a pressure gauge, you have a check on the amount of air available. And with a direct feed ABLJ you can adjust your buoyancy, or use it as a lifting device, and still know that you have sufficient air for an emergency ascent.

The disadvantages are complex. The jacket has to be connected to the aqualung cylinder via a tube of sorts, and this tube can split or puncture. Where the tube is taken from the high or low pressure part of the regulator, the restrictor device to prevent the air flooding out in the event of a ruptured hose is often removed to enable the jacket to fill quickly. Sometimes the restrictor is built into the regulator by virtue of the bore of the casing at this point. If this restrictor has a large throat, the jacket will inflate quite quickly when the aqualung cylinder is fully inflated, but very slowly when the cylinder pressure is low. It is often said, and by people who should know better, that the direct feed ABLJ cannot function if you run out of air in the normal way. This is not always true. Just because the diver can't suck any air through the mouthpiece at, say, 30 metres, it doesn't mean there is no air in the cylinder because, usually, if he ascends a few metres he can get another breath or two as the ambient pressure decreases; and this air will provide lift, depending on the regulator. If the regulator is very efficient it will use virtually the last scrap of air, leaving you with little or no 'lifting power', but if the regulator is one of those cheap and nasty models which can't function properly at 20 metres when you are starting on the red, then you will probably have more than enough lifting power left. So, from the safety angle the paradox is that the better the regulator the less safe is the direct feed ABLJ. I have tried several types of regulator with a direct feed ABLJ, at depth, and can vouch that in general the twin hose two-stage regulator is so efficient that you can breathe your air down to the point where there is little or no lift available for the jacket. On the other hand, many of the single hose, or twin hose single stage, regulators usually have enough air for ascent—even if the diver is gasping for air.

Some of the disadvantages of the direct feed ABLJ are:

(*a*) You have to remove the restrictor valve for optimum efficiency; and the restrictor is a safety device.

(*b*) If you suck your aqualung 'dry' at depth, you do not know how much—if any—lifting power there is left.

(*c*) Your feed tube must be checked frequently. If it ruptures you could be in trouble.

At this point you might have made a mental note that the safest system must be a direct feed ABLJ with separate cylinder attached. The 'hairy' divers might sneer at this combination of 'belt and braces', but at least it stops your trousers from falling down!

It must be mentioned that some regulators are so constructed that a direct feed ABLJ cannot be used properly.

This is usually the case when the regulator has some sort of restrictor device built into the mechanism.

There is no valid excuse for not wearing a suitable lifejacket when diving. Some people complain about the expense, but there are too many divers around with gleaming twin cylinders and tatty lifejackets—if worn at all. Far better to stick to one cylinder and a good lifejacket if price is the main consideration. And in the case of people who complain at the expense anyway, I can only say: If you can't afford the game, take up squash or something. We are dealing here with human life and every diver has the right to expect that his buddy, who would have to come to his assistance in an emergency, should be suitably equipped. So make the purchase of a good lifejacket a priority.

Don't forget:

Never use a cylinder ABLJ as a lifting device or buoyancy adjuster.

Never use any ABLJ as a means of getting to the surface other than in an emergency. The ABLJ lifts you to the surface at a speed that could bring on a burst lung, or decompression sickness, far easier than with a conventional ascent.

Ancillary equipment

Having obtained the essential equipment with regard to comfort, function and safety, the diver is confronted with a bewildering variety of instruments and mechanisms that possess varying degrees of utility. Their usefulness will depend on the individual—the diver working in conditions that cause him to become ensnared in ropes or cables would consider a knife an essential, while the diver performing dives that require decompression would consider a watch and depth gauge more useful.

Knife

A knife is the most popular 'extra', and serves many purposes. It will be used for prising, chopping, sawing, and, of course, cutting! It follows that it should conform to a general pattern of construction and design, because some of the knives on the market were never manufactured with underwater work in mind—these are mostly 'adapted' from the Scouting or kitchen range by some enterprising salesman and are ill suited to underwater work.

The 'floating' knife is rarely used by divers. It is a useful knife for the boat owner or fisherman, but a diver's knife must be of much more rugged construction; one that could be used, if necessary, as a lever. One edge should be serrated, and is used for cutting through heavy rope or cable, while the other edge should possess a plain, sharp cutting edge. A stainless steel blade will require less maintenance than hardened steel; the latter will rust if not permanently covered with grease. The handle should be large enough to grasp firmly while wearing bulky, foam-neoprene gloves, with a non-slip surface and a guard large enough to prevent the hand from slipping on to the blade.

The sheath needs to be of efficient design. High-density plastic, fibreglass, or metal are better than leather or fabric, both of which are of little use. Metal sheaths usually hold the blade by means of a strong spring attached to the inside, but metal sheaths are rarely seen nowadays. Plastic sheaths are the most popular, and often secure the knife with a small clip or band of elastic round the handle. This is fine, but it is often difficult to put the knife back in the sheath, and secure the clip/elastic when you are wearing thick gloves.

The position of the knife is one of individual preference. If worn at the waist, do not secure it to the weight belt; and make sure that if you have to release the weight belt it will not snag on the knife handle. Many divers strap the knife to the calf; this is quite convenient because the handle strap buckles round the leg just below the knee, and the lower strap round the ankle. In this position it is easy to reach for, or replace, the knife; and it's unencumbered by the equipment covering the torso.

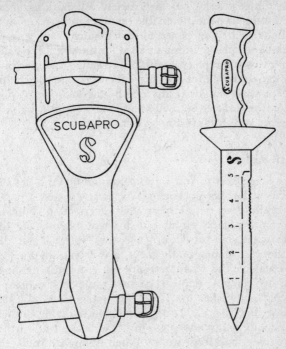

A heavy duty Scubapro knife.

Compass

The compass is indispensable for direction finding, or completing a detailed search or survey under water. When submerged, your sense of direction can deteriorate rapidly, and it is essential that a diver, particularly when at sea, should know in which direction the shore, or boat, lies.

The cheap, popular air-filled compass is of no use under water—it will fill with water or implode (the opposite to explode)—so it is essential that a compass for underwater

use be of the liquid-filled type. Apart from this consideration, the dial or card of a liquid-filled compass is more
steady than the jerky, air-filled variety. All markings should
be in luminous paint, to enable readings to be taken in the
dim light so often encountered under water.

Leather or plastic is usually used for the strap. If possible,
remove this and replace it with heavy-gauge elastic webbing
or an expanding bracelet. This will ensure that the compass
fits your wrist snugly at any depth; the solid strap will fit
well on the surface, but will hang loose at depth, when the
water pressure compresses the suit material.

Depth gauge

Every diver likes to know the maximum depth of his dive,
whether it has been a twenty foot or seven metre 'paddle'
or a really deep one. Experienced divers often claim that
they can accurately estimate their current depth, but these
boasts never stand up in practice, for if there is one thing
definite about human judgement, it is its variability. There
are times, such as when decompressing, when a method of
accurately judging depth is essential; and this is where the
depth gauge comes in. The depth gauge is rarely 100%
accurate, but is usually adequate for most diving purposes.
It is usually balanced for use in sea water, which is heavier
and denser than fresh water. When diving in fresh water,
or far above or below sea level, slight inaccuracies will be
obtained owing to the difference in the density of fresh
water and/or the change in atmospheric pressure.

The most expensive depth gauge is not always the best or
most reliable, and if dives deeper than 40 ft. or 12 metres
are not contemplated, and you are careful when using it,
the capillary depth gauge is probably the best value and
most accurate. This consists of a glass or Perspex tube, open
at one end and closed at the other. On immersion, water
enters the tube and compresses the trapped air—the greater
the depth, the farther the water will travel along the tube.

Readings are then taken along the air/water demarcation line in the same manner as a thermometer. Capillary gauges need most care when you first enter the water; never jump into the water when wearing one, because this causes a series of bubbles to form in the tube, making it impossible to read. Slide into the water smoothly, and as the gauge enters the water make sure that the open end points down into the water. This will prevent a small bubble of air escaping and ruining your readings. Also, ensure that there are no obstructions in the tube—even a drop of water can cause a wide error.

The other types of gauge—Bourdon tube and diaphragm system—are read off the dial by a sweep hand or needle. The cheaper models never seem to function accurately until a depth of around 50 ft. or 15 metres is reached (just the opposite of the capillary, whose accuracy decreases with depth), but are more accurate below these depths.

Some of the more expensive models have a maximum-depth-reached indicator; these can be used, in addition, on a sounding line for a pre-dive check if you have not got a depth indicator built into the boat.

Watch

A watch has many applications under water. It is essential for dives requiring decompression, or complicated direction finding—on the other hand, you may merely want to know the time.

The cheapest timepiece for underwater use is obtained by enclosing an ordinary watch in a waterproof housing, but the watch designed specifically for this purpose is far neater and more popular. Prices vary, but technology in this field has reached the point where most makes are reasonably reliable. Unfortunately there are still a high proportion of underwater watches that leak when new. So select one that has a good guarantee, and take it back to the shop immediately you see signs of condensation or moisture through the glass.

When selecting a watch for diving make sure it has luminous markings (light gets deceptively dim under water). A sweep second hand is essential for navigation purposes, and a rotating bezel round the outside for recording the start of the dive or decompression stop.

Torch

A torch is useful for browsing around wrecks, exploring nooks and crannies in the rock face, and for night diving it is essential.

In fresh water an ordinary household torch will function quite well when flooded—although this is obviously an emergency procedure—but the same does not apply in sea water, because the short-circuiting action of the salts results in no useable light. Also, if your reflector is plated this will strip off in seconds.

In the circumstances where artificial lighting is needed, something reliable is essential. There are several solid diving torches on the market, so try to afford an instrument designed for the job. The all-rubber torch is usually designed to be waterproof, and does not hold up very well under pressure, so such torches should never be used for underwater swimming.

In the circumstances where you need a torch, you can't afford to lose it; so make sure that the torch is secured to your wrist, or some part of your equipment such as the harness, by a length of cord.

Writing under water

For the purposes of recording or communicating under water, some form of writing material is often required. A writing slate or pad for underwater use can be purchased, but it is really better to make your own, because you can then make it to the size you require. An ordinary slate or glasspapered white plastic can be used, but if you only have clear plastic available, glasspaper one side and paint the opposite side with white paint (you write on the rough side).

In all cases the writing instrument is an ordinary lead pencil, which should be attached to the slate or pad with a short length of elastic or a clip.

Thermometer

Any ordinary thermometer can be used under water, and it is not necessary to pay a high price. If only approximate information is required, then the cheaper models will be quite adequate. But if the records are required for scientific purposes, then a thermometer such as the type used for colour photography—guaranteed plus or minus not more than half a degree—must be used.

The thermometer is best mounted on the edge of the writing tablet, which affords it some protection and makes it convenient for recording.

Is it essential?

If you encumber yourself with equipment that is unnecessary for that particular dive, you not only make the dive less comfortable, but some item might get in the way at a vital moment and constitute a danger. If the dive you are on does not require a writing pad, or depth gauge, or even watch, then don't carry or wear them. The good diver carries only equipment that is relevant to the dive in progress.

6

Basic Diving Techniques

The standard required

Local conditions, and the availability of suitable diving equipment, are responsible for differing approaches to techniques and training in various parts of the world. However, there is one cardinal rule that is universally approved by amateur divers: *never dive alone*. Disregarding this rule has accounted for many deaths, and, strangely, the blind acceptance of it has probably also been responsible for fatalities, because it is inadequately worded. It should really read: *never dive without an adequate partner*. An underwater companion who is always missing when needed, or who is poorly and inadequately trained, is not a suitable person to entrust your life to—and that is what it amounts to. It takes little to achieve a reasonable standard of competence: a sturdy finning action; proficiency in mask and hose clearing; practical knowledge of emergency procedures; and thorough familiarity with diving equipment and its dangers, are all that is required.

It is worth repeating that every diver is entitled to expect that his partner—who after all would have to come to his rescue—is capable of dealing with the average emergency.

Training

Your diving lessons should be carried out under the expert eye of a qualified diving instructor; but there are several points that we can discuss in advance, so that you can present yourself suitably primed.

The first stage of practical instruction will be on aspects of the aqualung. Before you enter the water, a check should be made to ensure that the cylinder is adequately filled, and the regulator is functioning correctly.

The first check is on the cylinder valve 'o' ring. Examine this to see that it is not cut or damaged in any way. If it is, replace it.

Next attach the regulator to the cylinder valve; the connection should be tightened by hand—never with a spanner or similar tool.

The contents of the cylinder are checked with the pressure gauge (if you only have a reserve system, you will have to employ an independent pressure gauge before you fit the regulator). Lay the fitted aqualung down and turn the glass-fronted face of the pressure gauge *away* from you, then turn the cylinder valve on. The set should ideally be left like this for about five minutes, before the gauge is picked up and the contents read. The reason for this sequence is because if there is a fault in the pressure gauge seals, it is sometimes possible for air to leak between the gauge face and glass front, causing it to explode after three or four minutes, or virtually immediately in some cases. This is in fact a very rare occurrence—I have only heard of it happening once in twenty-five years of diving—but if you have the time it is worth it, it is obviously pointless to take chances for the sake of a few minutes.

Having checked that the cylinder(s) is full, turn the cylinder valve off and watch the gauge carefully. The needle should remain firm at maximum pressure. If it drops steadily, there is a high-pressure leak—this could be at the cylinder valve washer connection, the gauge tube, or the regulator. If the needle fails to drop, place the mouthpiece in your mouth and suck out the remaining air. If you can still inhale a little air after the gauge needle has dropped to zero, a low-pressure leak is indicated, possibly at the point where the air-hose joins the mouthpiece or regulator.

Having assured yourself of the condition of your equipment, the first test will probably be the fitting on of aqualung, mask and fins while under water. This will consist of sinking your equipment, with the aid of a weight belt, then diving down (using a neat jack-knife dive), fitting the mouthpiece, laying the weight belt over your lap (to prevent yourself floating to the surface), adjusting and fitting the harness, clearing the mask, fitting fins, weight belt and snorkel, and returning slowly to the surface, exhaling steadily all the way. This test will prove quite easy if you have been practising fitting fins, mask and snorkel on in a single breath, as described in Chapter 2.

Other exercises, and tests, could consist of swimming along the bottom of a pool with your mask blacked out, to check on any possible claustrophobic tendencies, and/or sharing an aqualung under water, which will increase your confidence and breathing rhythm. The exercises and tests demanded by club or school are designed to lead you into aqualung diving with confidence, efficiency and safety. Don't try to avoid them, because maximum enjoyment comes with confidence in your ability.

A typical dive

On the assumption that nothing teaches better than practical experience, let us go through the motions of an imaginary dive, from start to finish. The location is a sandy beach set in a sheltered bay. It will be a shore dive, as no boat is available, and safety cover will be provided by snorkel divers. You are standing on the beach, in swimming costume, surrounded by (we hope) neatly laid out diving equipment, and you are a little apprehensive.

First clear up the jobs you can carry out before you climb into your bulky suit. You will have tested the cylinder(s) for contents long before you started out (at this stage it's pointless finding out you have no air), so now check the cylinder valve 'o' ring and replace if necessary. Open the cylinder valve for a brief second, to clear the orifice of any sand or moisture that may have accumulated. Next examine the regulator air filter for any similar accumulations, and connect the regulator to the cylinder valve. Turn the pressure gauge face so that it is pointing away from you, or anyone else, and open the cylinder valve. While waiting for the safety period to elapse, examine your lifejacket for possible tears or punctures. If the lifejacket is an ABLJ, check that the cylinder is full. This done, return to the aqualung unit, close the cylinder valve and check for contents and high-and low-pressure leaks. The test for a low-pressure leak will also enable you to 'taste' the air in case some 'odd' fumes might have entered during filling. After each inhalation through the mouthpiece, exhale slowly through your nose. This test will not enable you to assess positively whether the air is pure, but it is sometimes possible to detect excessively 'oily' air, or carbon monoxide fumes given off by a combustion engine.

After carefully donning your protective suit—wet or dry— it is important to observe certain priorities in fitting the rest of the equipment. It will be necessary to fit either the aqualung or lifejacket on first—the correct sequence depending on the particular construction of each. A lifejacket should not be covered by harness straps, but should be inflatable *over* them. A lifejacket fitted under the harness straps, and inflated, could crush your chest. When harness straps cross the chest, ensure that the lifejacket holding tapes are secured underneath them, so that if required you can jettison your aqualung but leave your lifejacket in place. Last of all comes the weight belt. This item must be placed over all other equipment, so that it can drop freely when the quick-release is pulled. This last point might seem obvious, but it is surprising how many divers enter the water with their weight belt strapped *underneath* their aqualung harness, making the belt quite impossible to jettison quickly.

Bring your mouthpiece into position, just under your chin, place the mask on your forehead, snorkel in place,

D

and fit auxiliary items such as watch, depth gauge etc. The fitting of fins depends on the distance from kitting-up to the point of water entry. If a fairly long walk is necessary, carry the fins and fit them at the water's edge; but in this case you are on a beach with immediate access to the water. On arrival at the water's edge, spit on the inside face of the mask, rub around and rinse to prevent misting. Get your buddy to turn on your air if you can't reach yourself.

Meanwhile the instructor, or dive leader, will be giving a pre-dive briefing: under water, you are to swim slightly behind him, on his right. The dive will take place along a rocky ridge some 200 yards or metres out, and to save air the outward journey will be made on snorkel. The final check is on weighting—you don't want to be heavy while swimming on the surface—and you are away.

As you snorkel out, mask buried in the water, the sea bed unfolds its mysterious landscape. Fronds of seaweed sway rhythmically in the mild wave surge and a purple, trans-lucent jelly-fish drifts lazily along. The bottom slopes gently away, and visibility is reduced to an opaque blue-green, when suddenly a rock finger points through the green velvet fog. You've arrived. Change over from snorkel to aqua-lung. The dive leader gives the O.K. sign, which is returned all round. A neat jack-knife dive and you are, for a while, in a world of fantasy.

At about 10 ft. or 3 metres, the water pressure becomes obvious on your ears; a gentle clearing motion and you are on your way down again. Down to 35 ft. or 10 metres, and you hit the bottom; and you become conscious of a little water in your mouthpiece. The method of eliminating this excess depends on the type of regulator you are using. With a twin hose model, turn sideways so that the exhaust hose (sometimes on the right, but more often on the left; a point that you should have noted in pool training) is located at the bottom or sea bed side, and the inlet hose towards the surface. Blow into the mouthpiece. Water in a single hose mouthpiece requires a different procedure. The centre of the mouthpiece contains a 'purging' button; pressing this activates the diaphragm and causes a burst of air. Of course, you will have been well drilled in these exercises before you go on a dive.

At the bottom, a further exchange of O.K. signals, and off you all go, you in particular keeping carefully on the right hand side of the leader. Now you can look around.

At your approach, a tiny hermit crab scuttles across the sandy bottom and, leaping into a shell several sizes too small, frantically claws the shell like a fat woman trying to struggle into a corset. A rocky outcrop sporting strap-like seaweed comes into view, and also a small colony of that colourful marine 'hedgehog', the sea urchin. The dive leader stops, and solemnly takes hold of your pressure gauge. With a start, you remember that you were supposed to inform him when the pressure dropped to 60 ats, then again at 30 ats. The reading is now 35 ats. Luckily you can't hear him muttering as he sets his compass sights for shore. The vegetation becomes more prolific as the floor slopes gently upwards. You concentrate on breathing steadily, taking care not to inhale deeply.

Back on shore, however tired you are, don't just throw your aqualung unit on the beach. Carefully remove the regulator from the cylinder, and pack each one neatly away, safe from gritty particles, along with the lifejacket.

The above dive, although described as typical, could, of course, have had several different permutations. A boat would have necessitated a vertical descent and ascent; the visibility could have been very poor, in which case you might have been joined to the leader by means of a 'buddy line'; or an emergency might have occurred.

On the surface

It cannot be repeated too often: an aqualung diver, laden with equipment, is most vulnerable when on the surface and out of air. There are several points that should be borne in mind—and practised—long before a long snorkel home in full kit is undertaken.

Always make sure that you are fractionally buoyant on the surface before you submerge. In case of error, you can always fall back on your weight belt quick-release; but don't wait until you are half-drowned before groping for the buckle. A common cause of trouble is the change-over from aqualung mouthpiece to snorkel, particularly in choppy water. You should practise the change-over, in training, until the procedure becomes second nature. It is common practice, among experienced divers who use a lifejacket possessing a mouthpiece, to partially inflate the jacket before commencing a long snorkel; this again is a procedure with which you should be thoroughly acquainted before attempting it on a dive.

A problem often debated is whether, if in difficulty on the surface, to inflate the lifejacket first or release the weight belt. Of course, if in acute difficulty you should use the quickest means—and this means the lifejacket (problems can occur with snagged or awkward belts). However, if you are merely very tired, and in no immediate distress, an inflated lifejacket can cause a lot of additional drag, and this alone can prove exhausting, particularly against a current. In these circumstances the weight belt should be released.

If a cylinder is worn too high in the harness, it will tend to push you down when on the surface; and if you are using a snorkel you don't want to be too low in the water. The answer, of course, is to fit the cylinder properly in the first place. But mistakes can happen, and if this occurs turn round and try swimming on your back. In this way more of the cylinder will be immersed and the water will take most of the weight, making the swim back a little easier.

The ascent

The normal ascent poses few problems. Steady, regular

breathing, with a shallow intake of air and a positive exhalation, and a speed of around 60 ft. or 18 metres per minute, will ensure a safe ascent. But what of an emergency? There are two methods of ascent in an emergency—free and assisted—both fraught with danger and both requiring detailed knowledge of the procedures.

In a free ascent, as the name implies, the diver, out of air, ascends rapidly on his own. The danger of ascending (apart from decompression sickness) is the possibility of damaging the lungs due to the rapid expansion of the air they contained at the start of the ascent. The procedure, should a free ascent be forced upon you, is to breath out steadily (not forcibly) all the way up, while trying to keep calm (this last, of course, is almost impossible, but panic consumes precious oxygen very quickly). It must be emphasized that several noteable authorities, including the Royal Navy, insist that a free ascent should *not* be practised in training, for the dangers inherent in any free ascent more than offset the knowledge gained.

However, we can safely simulate the procedure in a swimming pool, without an aqualung. Fitted with mask and fins, retire to the deep end. Take a single deep breath, jack-knife to the bottom, and swim towards the shallow end, exhaling gently and continuously through the mouthpiece of the snorkel. Don't attempt to *fight* the desire to breathe but rather last the distance by controlled relaxation. Don't overdo it and surface as soon as you feel uncomfortable. The distance underwater should not exceed 25 yards or metres, and someone (who can swim!) must keep an eye on you while you are under water.

An assisted ascent, as the name implies, means sharing one diver's air supply while ascending together. The situation and procedure run like this: A diver's air supply fails. He attracts his partner's attention, and signals, indicating that he requires air. The partner swims to his side, keeping slightly below him, and passes *up* his mouthpiece. The victim has little or no water to clear from the mouthpiece,

because the fact that the mouthpiece has been offered upwards ensures that air will be flushing through. Then, in
turn, each diver takes two breaths before returning the
mouthpiece. When a regular breathing pattern has been
established they ascend steadily, each holding the other
firmly with his free hand.

Of course it's never exactly like that. For instance the
example quoted is perfect for a two hose job, and although
suitable for a single hose, mention would have to be made
of the facility for using the purging button that this valve
has.

On paper this method of surfacing in distress seems very
workable. But it is also fraught with dozens of problems.
If you run out of air your partner might be a long way away,
or even out of sight (it happens); or he might be a 'nervous'
diver—novice or experienced—who just doesn't like parting
with his mouthpiece under any conditions. And despite
what your more experienced friends might tell you, there
are quite a few of these divers around.

Assisted ascent requires practice, lots of it, in the swimming pool, going up, down, sideways etc., with the divers
you are likely to be diving with. You will soon find that it is
easy to share while you are both static, but when moving
mistakes occur far too easily.

Should one or both divers be poorly trained in this
exercise, and an attempt at an assisted ascent—emergency
or otherwise—from depth, be attempted, an error is prob-
able, placing both of them in danger. In fact, if in the
slightest doubt, make a free ascent.

Another form of ascent is by using the inflation attach-
ment of your ABLJ lifejacket, if you have one. The advantages and otherwise of this form of ascent are better described in the section on Lifejackets.

Hand signals

Accurate basic communication between divers, and from

diver to lookout or vice-versa, is essential for several reasons. It ensures safer diving and prevents wasting time with confusing charades. The signals should be kept to simple, easy-to-read actions or poses, and while it is perfectly acceptable to develop some special ones for use within your club or group, the internationally recognized signals shown here should be learnt first; and nothing you invent should conflict with these:

You, me or *that.* With the index finger (or complete hand if wearing mittens) the diver points to himself, another diver, or a specific object, and indicates the person or object to which any subsequent signals refer.

Are you all right?/All is well. The thumb and index finger form a circle as illustrated (a), and can be used as a question or reply.

Stop. The hand is opened and the palm held outwards, flat, with fingers together. Just like a policeman on traffic duty.

Go up/I am going up. The fist is clenched, with the thumb extending upwards, towards the surface (c). This signal will usually be preceded by another, such as *you* or *stop.*

Go down/I am going down. The same as (c), except that the fist is inverted, with the thumb pointing down.

I have 30 *ats* (*bars*) *left in my cylinder/I am on reserve.* The fist is clenched and held at eye level, on the right hand side of the mask, with the finger knuckles facing the receiver of the signal (d).

Distress. The fist is waved in a semi-circle, from shoulder to shoulder, passing the front of the mask with each swing (b). It indicates that immediate assistance is required.

Danger. The hand is drawn across the front of the neck, in a cut-throat movement.

The diver/lookout/snorkel cover will also have to communicate at times. There are two basic signals here.

Are you all right?/We are all right. The arm is thrust straight up, with the thumb and index finger in the *all is well* position (e). Used as question or reply.

Distress, come and get me/Come back (*in*) *immediately.* The arm is outstretched and waved from side to side in a semi-circle (f).

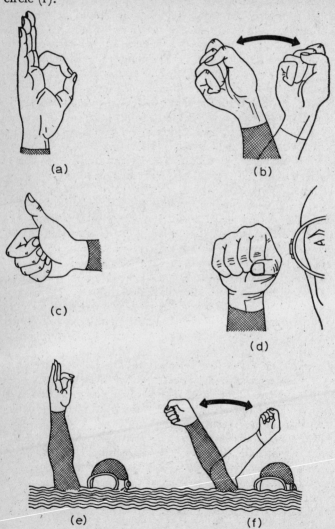

(a)

(b)

(c)

(d)

(e)

(f)

Underwater navigation

In some waters visibility will rarely exceed 20 feet or 6 metres, or even less. In these conditions the diver is unable to use some of the more directional aids such as fixing sights on a distant object. But as it is important that the diver should know the direction of the point of entry or shore, or the boat, for functional safety requirements, he has to adapt remaining aids to cater for underwater conditions.

Primitive navigation can be carried out by the observation of directional aids. A steady current, for example, will include much free-moving sediment that can easily be seen, creating a steady flow-line. The direction of the current can be fixed at the surface, giving an experienced diver a rough approximation of his position at all times. Using this method, tide tables should be charted in advance if applicable, for it is of little use if local currents should be turning, or variable. Sand ripples can also give a rule-of-thumb directional guide for the diver, as they will often run in the same direction for considerable distances. The usual method of swimming a non-compass course in a straight line is by sighting of objects in line. Three objects are sighted, say a large pebble nearby, a rock in the middle distance, and a patch of seaweed at the limit of vision. Ensuring that these items are really in line, the diver swims from pebble to rock, then looks for another object in line beyond the patch of weed, and so on. If three objects are kept continually sighted it is possible to swim in a remarkably straight line. Reverse the method for finding your way back. For diving on a flat, sandy bottom which is featureless, you should have a length of wood or metal (ten inches or 250 millimetres of broom handle is excellent) which is trailed by hand along the bottom as you swim out. This creates a narrow groove in the sand which you can use to easily find your way back to your point of entry.

A good liquid-filled compass is essential for detailed

navigation and search procedure, provided its drawbacks are known. Being magnetic, a compass is badly affected by metal objects in the vicinity, and the diver is well laden with metal—regulator, knife, buckles, cylinder (if of steel) etc. Provided the compass is always read with these objects in the same relative positions, these errors will remain constant and can be ignored. A more serious threat comes from objects that do not retain the same position and distance, such as your partner's equipment, the anchor chain, or a wreck. An important point to remember is that a compass does not take a bearing on an object; it can only give you a bearing in the line of which your object lies. For example, in the diagram the diver in position 1 could find his way back to the boat by following his compass reading of direct north. However, should a current carry him downstream to position 2, we can see that by following his

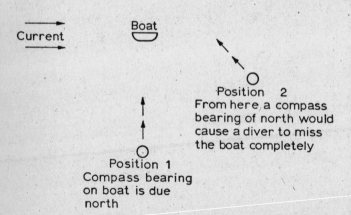

Magnetic north
N

Current

Boat

○
Position   2
From here a compass
bearing of north would
cause a diver to miss
the boat completely

○
Position 1
Compass bearing
on boat is due
north

The compass is almost always right, but the diver isn't.

compass reading of north he will miss the boat by a consider-able margin. Calculations to compensate for this can only, at best, be a guess, although experience and training can produce remarkable accuracy. Bad navigation can produce dangerous situations, so if there is the slightest doubt in your mind as to your position, surface immediately to check your bearings. In any case this should be done when your air supply falls to half pressure, and again when low, to ensure that you can make it back to base under water, without the necessity of a long, tiring swim back. Of course this only applies to a relatively shallow dive, you won't be bouncing up and down on a deep dive for obvious reasons but then, you won't be travelling very far either!

7

Advanced Diving Techniques

Roped diving

An aqualung diver is—subject to the limitations of time imposed by his air supply—unencumbered by attachments to the surface. Occasions occur, however, when safety and functional efficiency necessitate a positive connection to the surface. Among the advantages of a diver roped to the surface are: basic signals can be interchanged between diver and surface; the diver can be hauled to the surface if circumstances warrant it; should the diver become entangled in an obstruction, the standby diver can locate him immediately, even in conditions of zero visibility and light; the diver can locate his point of entry by returning along the rope, or by signalling to be pulled up.

In conditions that indicate roped connections, a companion diver is sometimes an encumbrance. Low-visibility roped diving is best carried out by an experienced solo diver, in conjunction with a surface tender who is well practised in this sort of work. Where a companion is a possible asset, e.g. under ice, the more experienced diver is roped to a surface line, and attached to his partner by a short wrist-to-wrist line (sometimes called a buddy line).

Because of the dangers of entanglement with one's own line, a sturdy, sharp knife should be carried by all divers, including the standby, who are participating. The knife should be secured to the sheath or belt (never to the weight belt) by a length of strong cord or elastic.

The surface line should be securely attached to the diver,

in a position well clear of equipment such as mask, regulator, any quick-release buckles etc. The line can be secured round the diver's waist, before he fits his harness, or it can be fastened to the harness. The rope should be fastened somewhere at the back, and from here, take it under the armpit of the signalling arm, along the forearm, and hold it with two turns round the hand. *Never* secure it by turns round the forearm or wrist.

Most of the advantages of roped diving—particularly in low visibility—are lost unless both diver and tender are well practised. Signalling with a surface line should be on the agenda during pool training or whenever you are diving in shallow water and have some time to spare.

Bear in mind that signals cannot be transmitted along a slack line. At all times the rope should be as taut as comfort will allow, so that both tender and diver can 'feel' one another. It is preferable that the surface tender is also an experienced diver; this will ensure that the tender can appreciate fully the possible difficulties of the submerged diver.

The line should be less than half an inch or 13 millimetres in diameter, but thick enough to grasp firmly, and capable of supporting a dead weight in excess of 500 pounds or 128 kilogrammes.

The following five signals should cover most requirements. You can develop more if you wish, but don't change the ones listed below.

Signal	Diver to surface	Surface to diver
One pull	I am O.K.	Are you O.K.?
Two pulls	I am stationary	Stay where you are
Three pulls	I'm going down	Go down
Four pulls	I'm coming up	Come up
Continuous pulls	Emergency	Emergency, pulling you up.

Low visibility

The cause of low visibility can be suspended sediment, poor light, or both. In any case, it is usually better for the diver(s) to be roped to a surface tender when the visibility has to be measured in terms of inches or centimetres. The limitations of visibility that necessitate a surface line will obviously vary with the experience of the diver(s). In general, when visibility is less than two feet or 60 centimetres, a diver is better off diving alone with a surface line. If visibility is better than this, diving can be carried out in pairs, the more experienced diver attached to a surface line and to the other diver by a 'buddy line' (see Roped diving). As the dangers of diving in water of low visibility includes entanglement with submerged items such as rope and wire, branches of fallen trees etc., essential equipment should include a knife and torch.

You should check yourself out for any possible claustrophobic tendencies by swimming around the pool with a blacked-out mask.

Under water, don't fin along in a hurry when vision is nil or low. Feel your way along slowly, to ensure that you do not swim into a submerged barrel, drum or tank. Also, surface slowly and carefully, with one hand extended upwards, otherwise there is a possibility of cracking your head against a boat, jetty, or a swimming or floating object.

Diving at night

Diving at night attracts an ever-growing group of enthusiasts. The underwater world is never exactly noisy, but at night the silence becomes positively eerie. The diver's torch cuts silver tunnels through black velvet water, and colours appear brighter, and more intense, in the light of a good torch. And fishes that normally keep their distance boldly thrust themselves into the paths of light.

It must be pointed out that much normal diving pro-

cedure is inapplicable to night diving. Signals obviously
suffer. On the surface, communication with the lookout can
only be a pre-arranged series of Morse-like torch signals.
Keep these signals short and simple to avoid confusion. All
that are basically needed are *All O.K.* and *Distress*. From
personal experience I have evolved the following signals
that have proved their worth for around twenty years now:
All O.K. Two short flashes (repeated several times). *Distress*.
A continual beam. With the O.K. sign, repetition is
required in case the lookout should miss the first. In the
case of the 'distress signal', the continual beam will enable
the rescuers to locate the distressed diver(s). In both cases,
the identical signal should be repeated from shore or boat.

Under water, the divers should keep strictly to pre-
arranged pairs, and each diver should keep in close contact
with his partner, for if your companion gets into trouble
and his light fails or is not turned on, it will be almost
impossible to find him in the dark. In fact it is better to be
joined wrist-to-wrist with a short buddy line.

The location of a night dive is of paramount importance.
In lakes and similar areas things will, with luck, go according to plan. But at sea a close check should be kept on tide
tables if it is a tidal location. A headland jutting out to sea
is a potentially dangerous hazard in daylight; at night, a
diver could be swept well away before the alarm is raised.
The best type of sea location is a sheltered bay when tides
are at neaps.

Diving under ice

It is doubtful whether diving under ice has as great a visual
attraction as night diving. Nevertheless this form of subaquatic activity has its devotees—they can be seen at the
bar, always drinking large measures and wearing purple,
balloon-sized goose-pimples!

Whatever the thickness of the ice, diving should always
be carried out in conjunction with a surface line roped to

the diver(s), and the line should not in any circumstances be paid out more than 25 feet or 8 metres if the dive is horizontal i.e. away from the entry hole. If the dive is vertical (straight down-and-up), on a weighted shot line, the line securing the lead diver might be paid out farther than 25 feet if the diver(s) is experienced.

Whether to wear a lifejacket is debatable. More lifejackets are inflated unnecessarily, in a moment of panic, than are inflated in genuine emergencies. While this is no great problem in normal conditions, under ice the diver, ascending the last few yards or metres at a considerable speed could, on hitting the underside of the ice, injure himself or dislodge some essential equipment. On balance it is probably inadvisable to wear a lifejacket under ice. A possible exception could be an ABLJ because this has the advantage that the diver can breathe from the jacket if the regulator stopped working—and under ice there is always a possibility that your regulator could freeze up. In any event, a diver should be very experienced before wearing a lifejacket under ice. On the other hand, it is fair to say that any diver venturing under ice should be experienced anyway.

Fast-moving rivers

Diving in swift, clear, river water can provide an exhilarating activity for well-trained and experienced divers.

Ropes are a dubious advantage. The danger of a diver, tumbling along, swept by the current, and becoming entangled and perhaps displacing some essential equipment is all too possible.

In these conditions it is best to swim against the current. This serves two purposes: the current can't get a 'grip' on you, and perhaps dash you against some rocks; and the mud churned up by your fins will be carried downstream, not along your line of vision.

Cave diving

Quite honestly, there is enough to see and experience under water to last a lifetime, without venturing into the dangers of cave diving. Pot-holing in air requires substantial skill, training and experience; under water, far more is required of all three, and in addition there is absolutely no margin for error. Scientific expeditions sometimes find it necessary to explore caves under water, but the only really good advice on cave diving that can safely be given to the amateur, pleasure-loving diver is—don't.

Of course this does not apply to the shallow excursion— no deeper than the distance you can fin on one lung full of air—into the inevitable cave you will chance upon. Even so, it is all too easy to go in too far. Cave diving, even the shallow kind, should never be undertaken without a line securely fixed to the diver and a 'tender' outside the cave or on the surface (see Roped diving). The diver should never be alone unless the visibility is nil, and a torch should always be carried. And standby divers (ready for instant action) should be ready.

Towing sledge or aquaplane

The towing sledge is really a cross between a surf-board, water-skis, and a sledge. In practice a board of marine plywood, approximately 6 ft. or 2 metres in length and 3 ft. or 1 metre wide is towed by a boat, with a diver reclining on its uppermost surface. The board can ascend and descend via manually operated flaps, and sometimes a 'waterscreen' is built on to protect the diver from the self-imposed 'current'.

The sledge is ideal for searching large areas of clear water quickly. The lack of exertion enables the diver to extend his air supply and, consequently, his time under water. Nonetheless, the aquaplane is no vehicle for the novice diver. The rider has a considerable force of water

E

pressing against him because of his forward momentum, and the possibility of this force dislodging his mask is always present. Also, the aquaplane is capable of ascending more steeply than is apparent to the human eye, with the accompanying danger of embolism; so when the planing flaps are in the 'up' position, pay especial care and if possible regulate breathing to shallow breaths. When ascending in order to surface, breathe out as in a free ascent unless a gradual upward plane can be gauged accurately.

Never ride an aquaplane when visibility is poor, there is always the danger of collision with some object you will see too late. The rider should never be tied or in any way secured to the aquaplane; the mere act of releasing his grip should be enough to release him from the board.

Underwater scooter

Much relating to the aquaplane also applies to the underwater scooter. The scooter is usually an electric propulsion device for towing a diver either on the surface or under. It has the advantage over the aquaplane in that the speed can be regulated instantly, and there is no dependence on a surface unit or connection.

One of the dangers of the scooter is its ease of transport; it is all too easy to travel a long distance, but what do you do if it breaks down far from home? For this reason alone it is best for scooter riders to travel in pairs of scooters.

Wrecks

Diving on wrecks is without doubt the most popular diving activity; there is the thrill of exploring a sunken vessel, but this carries with it the dangers carried in such exploration—and then there's the legal aspect, which varies from country to country. The latter is of great importance, because there is always the temptation to recover objects from a wreck and take them home, or to the clubhouse, as souvenirs.

Every wreck, or part of it, has a legal owner who is still entitled to the remains of the wreck, including the cargo. Any person who removes part of a wreck with the intention of depriving the legal owner of possession, is committing an offence. The punishment, if one is convicted of such an offence, varies from country to country but usually includes imprisonment.

Of course, there is usually nothing to prevent you just looking, and wreck hunting and diving lay claim to the largest group of enthusiasts in any aspect of underwater activity. Wrecks usually contain prolific marine growths, and serve as home to a wide variety of fish. A knowledge of the history of a sunken vessel, including the events leading up to the disaster, can make the dive that much more interesting. If the wreck is indicated on an Admiralty chart, the Hydrographic Department can sometimes give you some details, for a fee. If the name, and year of sinking are known, the Shipping Editor of Lloyds can probably fill in the rest of the picture—again for a fee. Don't forget the local newspapers, they often contain news of sinkings in the locality, but you'll have to know the approximate date of sinking. Wreck research is almost as fascinating as wreck diving, and is something you can do during the winter months.

It cannot be emphasized too strongly that all wrecks are potentially unstable, and there can be little or no warning should one move, or a section capsize. For this reason it is not wise to enter a wreck without the most stringent precautions, and only by experienced divers. A good torch is essential when looking over most wrecks, as there will be many dark corners to peer into. Don't thrust your hands into these cavities—a conger, moray or crab might take exception! Rusting parts will, in time, corrode to the thickness of a knife edge, and there is plenty of metal on most wrecks, so be careful when you are climbing around a wreck or you might surface with some nasty gashes.

If you are looking for a very old wreck, bear in mind

that it might no longer look like a ship. Years of collapse and a thick growth of seaweed and other marine organisms might have completely covered any obvious features. In this case look for features that are not natural, such as a straight line. In nature, few things are really straight, unlike man-made things like masts, cannon, planking etc., so if anything under water runs in a straight line it is worth investigating.

8

Sea Diving

Dive planning and procedure

Whatever the cause it is a fact that, apart from choosing the date and general location, diving expeditions are often very inadequately planned. Such an approach will rarely enable the participants to obtain the maximum enjoyment from the dive—and this is apart from the aspect of safety—and, as a result, enthusiasm can soon pall.

An emergency is the time when the real value of advance planning is shown. Thus the first items of information to obtain are the addresses and telephone numbers of the nearest doctor, hospital, coastguard, and recompression chamber. The first two will probably be easier to obtain on arrival at the diving location, but the latter pair should be obtained in advance.

A nautical chart of the area is indispensable to any well-planned diving expedition. Research on coastal features, depths, tides (if applicable), wrecks, restricted or dangerous areas, quality and type of bottom etc., can be carried out in advance, saving valuable time. Having obtained the chart, mark off any potentially interesting sites. Reefs and rocky outcrops usually prove most interesting, often abounding in fish life and lost anchors, as do wrecks.

The Admiralty publish an annual catalogue of their nautical charts, and these cover the whole world. Any study of nautical charts requires a knowledge of the symbols and abbreviations used, and in the case of Admiralty charts this information is available on a special chart—

number 5011—issued for this purpose. But also take a look at some of the nautical charts published by private companies, they are usually more colourful and there might be features that you prefer.

The next pre-dive check is on tide tables, if you are diving in a tidal area. If possible your dive should coincide with a period of slack water, and this usually (but not always) occurs at the time of maximum high or low tide. High tides usually provide better underwater visibility, especially when diving near the coast, because the deeper, clearer waters are 'flooding' in, whereas when the tide is ebbing out it often takes with it the coastal sediments and muds.

If possible choose a date on which a neap tide occurs. Neap tides present the least rise and fall in water level, and create proportionately less water movement, giving longer slack water periods.

Having decided the approximate time you will be diving, examine the chart for tidal stream data. Currents vary greatly in speed at different times of the tide, and some sites experience dangerous waters even when the area in general is at a slack period.

The telephone usually provides information on weather conditions in specific parts of the country, and a call, just before you leave, might save an otherwise wasted journey, because good weather at home does not rule out a force four wind blowing a hundred miles away.

On arrival at the dive location, obtain from the harbour master any information regarding restricted or banned areas, and the fairways used by local boats—these should be avoided. Also, inform the harbour master where you intend to dive and if you possess, as you should, distress signals, tell him the form they take.

The tides

In sea diving it is important to possess a basic knowledge of tides and their behaviour, for only then can you appreciate the advisability of diving at pre-calculated times. In virtually land-locked area such as the Mediterranean, tides are no problem to the diver as the difference between high and low tide is less than twelve inches or 30 centimetres, but in places like Britain and America, where the tidal range can vary in places from several feet or a couple of metres to a gigantic pile-up 50 feet or 15 metres high, it pays to afford tide tables a little attention.

The tides are periodic vertical movements of the seas, and are brought about by the gravitational pull of the Moon and the Sun. The most powerful influence is that exercised by the Moon. This has the effect of drawing water towards the face of the Earth nearest the Moon and creating, in fact, a 'bulge' in the depth of the water at that point. This accumulation is duplicated on the opposite side of the Earth, and when either of these 'bulges' passes a specific area, high tide occurs, and it can be seen that at any time there are two continual high tides traversing the surface of the world. Conversely, either of the flattened 'troughs' that lie between the bulges constitutes a low tide.

As if this were not enough, we then have the gravitational pull of the Sun to contend with. The Sun, owing to its greater distance from Earth, exerts a gravitational pull only half as powerful as that of the Moon. Nonetheless it does exert a 'magnetic' attraction on the seas. When the Sun and Moon are in line—that is, when the Moon is full, or new—the gravitational pull on high tide is intensified and is known as a spring tide (nothing to do with the time of year). When a spring tide occurs the waters rise higher, and fall lower, than usual. The greater mass of water flooding and ebbing causes tidal streams to flow faster, and this of course creates difficulties for the diver who has to swim against the currents.

The opposite effect is encountered when the Sun and Moon are at right angles to each other during the first or third quarter of the Moon. Their respective attractions tend to cancel each other out, creating a neap tide. This results in a minimum rise and fall in sea level; the advantages of diving during neap tides have already been described.

Calculating a high tide period is achieved by adding or subtracting a certain length of time from the high tide period of a specific area, known as a tidal constant. For example, using the times of high water at London Bridge, England, as our tidal constant, we find that high water at Southend is minus one hour and twenty-five minutes from the time quoted for London Bridge, while for Weymouth we would have to add five hours and five minutes. The time of low water will be approximately halfway between two consecutive high water times. Tables of tidal constants, relative to high water at various points around the coast, are published in many newspapers and in all nautical almanacs.

Unfortunately, it's not quite that easy, because tidal predictions can be thrown out because of the weather. Tides move round the world in a west-east flow, so that if a wind blows from the east for long enough this can slow down the tide, and if it blows from the west the high/low tide will arrive earlier than expected. So in addition to working out the optimum time for diving according to a set formula, you should also enquire locally in case tides are arriving earlier or later.

When two tidal streams converge—usually just off a point of land—a condition known as a race occurs. Races are well marked on nautical charts, and can often be seen as a broken, often frothy, patch when the rest of the surface is calm. Races are avoided by most vessels, and should be similarly treated by divers.

From shore or boat

The majority of sea dives are carried out direct from shore, because a boat, although desirable, is not always available —or is too expensive.

When diving from shore, select a spot that has an easy entry to the water, and with several similar points of return. A stretch of coast that has only one point of entry and return might necessitate a long, tiring swim back, and in a very strong current this might prove impossible.

The greatest emphasis should be placed on the diver's return to shore. It is not difficult to enter even a comparatively rough sea, but a diver chilled and exhausted, hampered by slippery rocks, surging waves, and laden down with equipment, can find the exit a hazardous procedure.

A danger to divers, particularly along breakwaters, is the hook and line of the angler with its threat of laceration and entanglement. Although no sensible diver would enter the water in the vicinity of anglers, the angler might appear on the scene after you have submerged. At a time like this your knife is your best friend. If hooked, cut your way out quickly, and don't try to emulate the antics of a fish—the fish hardly ever wins, anyway.

A shore base should be established that is comfortable for those who are not diving at that moment. A lookout frozen by biting winds is not capable of carrying out his job efficiently. Make sure that all the equipment is located above the high water mark, and that the lookout or another member of the shore party has a loosely coiled length of rope with a float attached; this can be thrown to any diver who is experiencing difficulty in landing.

A boat gives the diver access to a great number of sites, and for our purposes we can classify diving boats into two types: A dinghy, which is used for short excursions, where its occupants take their seats fully kitted-up owing to the shortage of space in which to move; and secondly, any larger vessel that permits the divers to change on board and, of course, has a greater range.

Considering the cardinal rule 'Thou shalt not dive alone', any boat should have a minimum complement of three —two divers plus one lookout/boatman—although this

arrangement is only advisable when diving close to shore
and in relatively shallow water.

The inflatable dinghy with an outboard motor is an
admirable boat for short distance work in calm water.
Virtually unsinkable, it lies low in the water, enabling returning divers to ease themselves aboard without much
danger of capsizing the vessel. It is so compact when de-
flated that it can be carried in the boot of a car, and when
home it can be stored in a small space—both extremely
useful features, especially to someone who lives in the city.

On a larger boat much more can be done to make diving
safer and more enjoyable. The equipment should be stowed
with separate compartments or places for wet and dry gear.
The same applies to cylinders; one stowage space should be
allocated for full cylinders and another, as far away as
possible, for empty cylinders. A most useful acquisition
would be a sturdy, rigid diving ladder that can be attached
to the gunwhale, and should be held out from the sides by
some sort of framework to enable a diver with fins on to
walk up it quite easily. Ensure that the bottom rung is
always well under water and securely tied, because a loose
ladder can flail around and injure a diver or damage the boat.

Other craft in the vicinity are always a possible danger,
so always fly the appropriate flag or flags to warn them off.
But bear in mind the fact that week-end sailors are a little
weak in their knowledge of flags, and if possible you should
have a loudhailer available so that a verbal warning can be
given. It has been known for an ignorant but otherwise
enthusiastic boatman to approach a diving boat—right over
the heads of the divers below—to ask 'What does that flag
mean?'

Lines should be rigged along the boat, so that divers can
hang on while resting, talking, or handing up equipment.
When you swim back to the boat after a dive, always pass
up your heavy gear—weight belt and aqualung—to make it
easier to climb aboard. Of course if you have a really large
boat and a good ladder this isn't necessary.

A potential hazard to divers is the screw or propellor. Even when in neutral, some screws tend to 'creep', so shut the engine off completely when the divers are in the water unless a good cage is attached round the screw.

Whenever possible hang a shot line, heavily weighted, next to the ladder. Divers can then ascend to the point of embarkation, eliminating a swim round the boat.

Also, in an emergency the anchor, if fouled, may have to be slipped quickly, so ensure that a buoy is fastened outboard on the boat end of the anchor line.

A long snorkel back to the boat can be an exhausting experience at the end of a dive. If a current is flowing, dive upstream on the outward journey, then you can get a free ride back! Whenever divers have to operate downstream from the boat, secure a float to a long line. The line can then be streamed aft until it is placed over the divers, and on surfacing the divers can hold the float or line and be hauled in.

Flag signals

The main use for flag signals is to prevent other vessels from sailing over the area where divers are operating. The trouble with this is that some sailors just don't know the recognized signals—for anything. Nevertheless the appropriate flag should be flown at all times because many sailors are aware of the various signals.

Fortunately, there is a flag in the International Code of Flag Signals (A) that means 'I have a diver down; keep well clear at slow speed'. This flag is used and recognized by most diving organizations around the world, but unfortunately not by the Americans, who still insist on using a red flag with a diagonal stripe in preference to International Code 'A' which is a white and blue swallow-tail. The main argument for the American flag hinges around the fact that red is a more visible colour, but the British Sub Aqua Club produced a survey several years ago that

International code of signals
Flag A

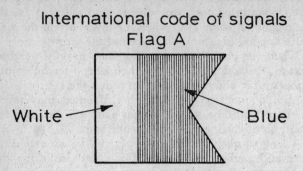

White → ← Blue

USA diving flag

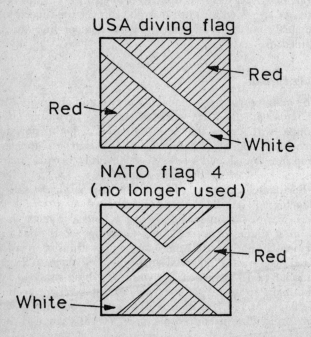

Red

Red

White

NATO flag 4
(no longer used)

Red

White

showed that too many flags use reds and the result is total confusion. And that a good blue is virtually as good. Bearing in mind the fact that virtually every diving organization in the world recognizes flag 'A' as the diving flag, and that it is a recognized shipping flag, it must sadly be assumed that commercial interests keep American divers flying their own individual flag that is out of keeping with the rest of the world.

Prior to the International Code designating flag 'A' as a diving flag, much of the diving world used the Nato 4 flag, which is red with a white cross of St. Andrew, which indicates that 'submarine operations are in progress'. The trouble is that even fewer people know the Nato Code than the International one. Nato 4 should never be used as a diving flag—there is enough confusion as it is.

A diving flag should be displayed clearly. It should be hoisted when diving commences, kept flying while the divers are down, and taken down when diving is finished.

9

Inland Diving

Although inland or fresh water diving cannot hold comparison to a good sea dive, it has many compensations and avenues of interest. The sea is a fickle creature, capable of many moods, and a long journey to the coast can be quite disappointing as you stand on the shore watching a force four wind blow up suddenly, ruining the day's diving. Also, many divers live too far from the coast to contemplate regular sea diving. Conditions at inland sites are more predictable, because most lakes, quarries and reservoirs have little or no currents, and the problem of selecting the period of slack water does not exist.

Stable conditions like these are ideal for training, as they offer the novice a natural progression from swimming pool to sea diving. Inland sites also provide winter diving sites when the sea is impossible to dive for months on end. There is also much work that can be carried out in scientific fields. Many lake beds have never been visited by divers, and are usually rich in legend; in Wales there is a 'sunken city' in Lake Bala, a 'monster' in Lake Glaslyn . . . and of course Scotland has Loch Ness. . . .

The most popular inland sites are flooded quarries or gravel pits, and lakes. A little diplomacy may be necessary when applying for permission to dive because angling clubs have snapped up fishing rights to most of the more interesting sites and tend to take objection to divers.

Lakes

In lakes, underwater visibility is usually adequate, though it can be a little murky where inlet streams or rivers feed the lake, but away from these sources visibility is normally in the region of around 14 feet or 4 metres.

A lake bed is usually composed of an intriguing combination of rotting leaves and other vegetation, and mud. The slightest movement will cause this soft sediment to billow up in dense clouds, reducing vision to inches or centimetres for a considerable time. So if another part is following you, or you think you might have to double back, or across, your path at some point, it is best to swim about 6 feet or two metres above the bottom of the lake and touch down only when you sight something of interest.

Lakes are often surprisingly deep. In rocky or limestone areas, vegetable and animal life is often scarce, and the clearness of the water enables light to penetrate down for a considerable distance, but in areas of softer land formation, prolific flora and fauna cause particles of matter to be released into the water and, along with other suspended sediment, filter the light on its downward journey. If the depth is considerable, complete darkness will envelope the bottom no matter how bright the sun is shining above. In these conditions torches are a must, and divers should be roped, either together, in pairs (via a wrist-to-wrist 'buddy line'), or singly, on a line to a surface tender (see 'Roped diving'). In lake diving the danger of swimming into the branches of a submerged tree is very real.

On lakes used for boating, always dive in conjunction with a surface dinghy following your bubbles to warn other boats away. Show the diving flag on the dinghy and verbally warn approaching craft away. In any case, lakes are often a deceptive distance in area, and even if the lake is not used for boating it is wise, especially with inexperienced divers in the party, to use a dinghy. A float (a car inner tube will do), directed by a snorkel swimmer, that a tired diver could use to take a breather, is a useful item.

On a more cheerful note, there is always the chance of stumbling on a 'wreck'. This might only be an old rowing boat in the last stages of decay, but it could be a larger and more recent submergence, in which case you can proceed with salvage negotiations.

Bear in mind that the edges of lakes have always been popular picnic grounds, and people throw the strangest things away. Make enquiries in the locality. If you can be reasonably sure that a particular site by a lake has been used for picnics and the like for many years it is always worth a dive. I started my bottle collection by diving in a Welsh lake that held dozens of old lemonade bottles at one corner. A local newspaper reporter explained this by the fact that this particular part of the lake had been extensively used for bardic ceremonies in Victorian times.

Reservoirs

Reservoirs are often useful diving sites, providing considerable surface areas of water and sometimes good depth. The constant turnover of water usually means a larger amount of suspended sediment, and proportionately reduced visibility, except in the case of very large reservoirs, which can be treated in much the same way as lakes. Indeed, many reservoirs are in fact converted from natural lakes.

Swimming of any kind is usually banned in direct drinking reservoirs, but sometimes allowed in other types, so ensure that permission is obtained before diving takes place. Also, check with the engineer regarding the position and flow of the outlet valves and any other potential hazard.

Canals

The canal is usually prolific in aquatic life, but the very presence of luxurious plant growth and fish life is of very little interest to the diver when vision is reduced to a couple of inches or centimetres, and this is often the case. Canals are universally regarded as a rubbish dump, thus the possibilities of encountering rusting bedsteads or bicycle frames—allied to zero visibility—can constitute a danger to the most experienced diver. When visibility is bad it is usually better to cancel a dive, and this applies particularly to canals. Canals that are no longer used sometimes have clear water and provide an interesting dive, especially if the diver has an interest in, and knowledge of, biology —or junk. The shallow depths enable a considerable amount of time to be spent under water, and a lot of research can be carried out in these man-made waterways. Again, don't forget to apply for permission. However poor the state of the canal, it belongs to someone.

Quarries and gravel pits

Flooded quarries and gravel pits are popular training sites for diving clubs. Access to the water is usually convenient, and if 'diving rights' are obtained the owner will sometimes allow changing facilities to be installed. These rooms can be used for lectures etc., after the dive.

If the quarry or pit is still being worked, visibility will usually be hopeless. But if work is not in progress reasonable conditions can exist. Like canals, such sites are favoured for rubbish disposal and can contain even larger items of danger, such as cars.

Rivers

Rivers that possess strong currents and poor visibility rank among the most dangerous of diving locations—the Thames in England is one example—along with swift-moving mountain waters, and these are dealt with in Chapter 7. However, rivers in non-industrial, rocky areas sometimes contain deep clear pockets or pools, below a waterfall for example, or on the outside of an acute bend in the river, which can provide good year-round diving.

Fresh water has a buoyancy index different to that of sea water, and in practical use this means that a weight belt balanced for a sea dive will need 2–3 pounds or 1 kilogramme of lead removed before a fresh water dive.

Although inland waters abound with a great variety of edible fish, it is important to note that in most countries there are regulations forbidding the taking of fish with a spear and/or underwater equipment. For example, in Britain the Salmon and Freshwater Fisheries Act of 1923 renders it illegal to use 'A spear or like instrument for the purpose of taking salmon, trout or fresh water fish'; and just you try catching them with your bare hands!

10

Rescue and Life Saving

Accidents and difficult situations can befall even the best planned diving expedition, for water is an alien medium for man to work in. Even on the surface of the water the aqualung diver, encumbered as he is by weighty equipment, is very vulnerable, probably more so than any other type of swimmer. So it is essential that divers can perform the correct type of rescue, and life saving, should conditions demand it.

The method of rescue and kind of treatment afforded the distressed diver depends on a quick assessment of the circumstances by the rescuer. Condition of the subject, distance and time required for getting him back to shore or boat, ease with which he can be towed, ease of landing the subject, all have to be taken into account in the briefest possible time: a few seconds delay—in calculating or carrying out the action—can mean all the difference between life or death.

Life-saving societies around the world do magnificent work in furthering the teaching of life saving. Anyone connected with a water sport should study their national life saving society handbook; and attempt to obtain one of the awards granted by many of them.

In addition to standard rescue and treatment methods, the underwater swimmer requires further techniques, particularly in the field of rescue, that are applicable to the modern aqualung diver.

Methods of rescue

Should a diver lose consciousness under water, his life will depend on his companion or buddy being able to carry out quick, efficient rescue drill. The rescuer should grasp the subject firmly by an arm, just above an elbow, removing *first* the victim's weight belt, and then his own. (If the procedure is reversed, there is the danger of the rescuer floating immediately upwards while the victim remains on the bottom). During the ascent, which should be smooth and steady, ensure that the victim is breathing out, or that the expanding air in his lungs is escaping. Should there be no sign of air coming from his lips or the regulator exhaust, press his stomach and ensure that it does. If one or both of you are wearing lifejackets, then whether they should be used depends on the degree of difficulty you experience in raising the victim. If possible you should just try to jettison weight belts and surface by fin power, because this will ensure a smoother journey up. However, if things are really urgent—for example if the victim has lost his mouthpiece and you can't get it back into place—then you will want to surface as quickly as possible. This means blowing at least one lifejacket; but the same applies as for the weight belts, don't blow *your* lifejacket first, otherwise you might drift upwards before you can do the same for the victim. There again it also depends on the type of lifejacket being used. The SLJ is virtually useless at depth while the ABLJ requires training in its use for maximum efficiency. Read the section on lifejackets very carefully in addition to the above.

So whether to inflate a lifejacket while under water depends on the circumstances; if the rescuer is in full control of the unconscious diver, then it is probably better to wait until the surface has been reached. On surfacing, at least the victim's lifejacket should be inflated, if he has one, using the automatic inflation mechanism. Unless he can be landed *immediately*, mouth-to-mouth should be attempted on the spot if he is no longer breathing. This of course takes some getting used to. After all, if you are both in the water and you have inflated the victim's lifejacket, it's a bit of an effort to apply mouth-to-mouth resuscitation. The obvious thing to do is to practice it—without actually doing it of course, for health reasons—at odd times when you are in the pool, or during a dive.

A person who is on the surface and in distress is a different proposition. Even a small person can be a dangerous handful when panic-stricken and struggling. Caution is required at all times; the victim might seem quite calm as you approach, only to burst into frenzied activity when you reach grasping distance.

When swimming out to attempt a rescue, it is important to keep your head out of the water with your eyes fixed on the victim. If your gaze should be diverted—even for a second—it is odds on that he will disappear under water at that precise moment, and you will waste precious time guessing where he went down. Also, never approach a distressed swimmer or diver from the front; do so carefully, from behind, and grasp him securely by the arms just above the elbows, holding him in this position until he has calmed down and is ready for a tow.

The method of towing depends on the condition of the victim. If he is calm, and he is wearing an inflated lifejacket, he could lay on his back and place his hands on the rescuer's shoulders, who could then fin forward in the usual manner. However, if the victim has no lifejacket this method could prove hazardous in the event of a sudden panic. In these circumstances, the rescuer should grasp the victim by the elbows while propelling him home. The important point is never to get into a position where the victim can grasp you fully.

Artificial respiration

Hundreds of years ago there was a strange method of

artificial respiration in vogue. It consisted of blowing air into the lungs, via a nostril, with a pair of bellows.

The ensuing years saw many 'superior' systems evolve. In Laborde's system, the victim's tongue was gripped between the folds of a handkerchief, jerked forward, then allowed to return to the mouth; this was repeated 15–20 times each minute. The Silvester method required manipulation of the victim's arms while he was stretched on his back. A Shafer method graduate, on the other hand, placed the victim face down and kept up a steady pressure on the back in the region of the lower ribs.

Currently the expired air method or mouth-to-mouth resuscitation—referred to in the popular Press as the 'kiss of life'—is considered the most efficient. The procedure here is for the rescuer to place his mouth over the victim's, while pinching shut the latter's nostrils, and to blow air into his lungs. It can easily be seen that the expired air method is, in principle, identical to the first method devised hundreds of years ago—except that the ancient method had an element of sophistication by the introduction of the bellows. It has taken mankind a couple of centuries to appreciate the efficiency of this aged system.

The expired air method is of particular importance to the diver. When a person has ceased breathing, it is essential that artificial respiration be carried out without delay; a long tow back to land or boat could prove fatal. The expired air method is the only procedure that permits artificial respiration to be carried out while victim and rescuer are still in the water.

The normal technique for carrying out expired air resuscitation is as follows: Place the victim on his back so that his chest is slightly higher than his stomach; ensure that his mouth is clear of obstruction and tilt his head well back; place your mouth over the victim's, seal his nostrils by pinching with your finger and thumb, and blow into his mouth. After exhaling, turn your head to see whether his chest is falling (if it is not, check that the mouth and throat are free of obstruction and try again). When starting, give a half-dozen quick inflations, reducing gradually to fifteen per minute.

Expired air resuscitation

Small children and babies require a slightly modified expired air technique, because hard blowing can damage their lungs. The rescuer can probably cover the baby's mouth and nose at the same time, avoiding having to pinch its nostrils. Respiration is carried out at the rate of 20 *gentle* puffs per minute; never blow violently into a baby's lungs.

The expired air system will introduce life-saving oxygen into the lungs at a better rate than any manual method, and is the method of artificial respiration preferred by most life saving organizations.

In training, never practise mouth-to-mouth resuscitation on another person by actually going through the procedure of blowing into their lungs. The risk of spreading infection will more than offset the benefit of the technique gained.

External heart massage

If, in addition to the cessation of respiration, the heart has stopped, then external heart massage should be given as soon as possible. This is ideally carried out by two operators, one applying expired air resuscitation and the other external heart massage. Should there be only one operator— and this is too often the case—then one inflation of the victim's lungs by the expired air method should be followed by ten heart compressions as follows. In the case of children it is sometimes possible for one person to work the procedure: Lay the victim on a firm, flat surface, face up.

External heart massage

Place the heel of the palm of one hand, with your other hand on the top of it, over the lower half of the breast bone (sternum). Rock forward, using your weight to exert a pressure that will depress the breast at least an inch; rock backwards, decreasing the pressure. Repeat at a rate of 60 compressions per minute, (slightly faster, and with much less pressure, for children). In the case of a baby use only two fingers, applying sharp but gentle pressure.

As with expired air resuscitation, external heart massage should never actually be practised on another person in training. A couple of broken ribs—of little consequence to the casualty whose heart has stopped beating—can be rather annoying to the person being used as a dummy.

And of course it's not really as easy as all that, although the above is better than nothing in an emergency. You should really contact your local first aid or life saving society and obtain competent instruction in these methods. And bring along your diving partner—he may have to use it on you one day!

11

Photography Under Water

A photographic record of your activities is a rewarding and pleasurable possession in any sport or activity. And this is particularly true of underwater swimming because the underwater world is in many respects a photographer's dream. Unexplored scenery opens up in every direction; sometimes the vista will be suggestive of a science fiction landscape, and some of its inhabitants are just as bizarre. Spectacular rock formations, seaweed jungles, the delicate, translucent colours of the jelly-fish, the eerie majesty of a long-forgotten wreck—they all cry out to be photographed.

Subaquatic photographic apparatus has developed rapidly in the past decade, after a stumbling start, and the field of underwater photography, formerly the domain of the specialist, is now available to anyone with the patience to acquire the technique. It is not possible, in a single chapter, to cover fully a subject as vast and complicated as underwater photography, but a summary of basic essentials can be given that will guide the preliminary attempts of the underwater swimmer and help cut down the proportion of failures.

Although photographic equipment has reached a far higher standard than that available a few years ago, some of the difficulties in underwater photography are insoluble at present, and will probably remain so. Visibility under water is comparable to that of a permanent fog on land, sometimes vision can extend to 100 feet or 30 metres, and at other times be reduced to a few inches or centimetres. Suspended matter, in the form of mud, silt, plankton and other particles, causes this. There is no practical way of eliminating this 'fog', thus it becomes necessary to adapt photographic technique to prevailing conditions. The same can be said of the absorption of colours under the water—but more about this later.

The evolution

The 1890's saw the birth of underwater photography. At this time several people, in different countries, were experimenting, with the intention of obtaining photographs of the underwater world. The first to achieve success was Dr. Louis Boutan, a French biologist, who in 1893 obtained some fuzzy underwater stills. Boutan was not satisfied with these attempts, and continued experimenting with cameras of his own design, overcoming problems that were unknown to photographers of the time, and this culminated in the success of sharp photographs that have survived to the present day. The year 1900 saw the publication of Dr. Boutan's book *Progress in Undersea Photography*, almost certainly the first book on the subject. Book collectors should note that it was printed in French.

As with all dedicated scientists, the primitive tools he had to work with impeded Boutan—but never defeated him. There was no high-speed film available, Boutan had to use clumsy, fragile glass plates coated with wet collodion, and these necessitated exposures in the region of fifteen minutes. The camera was housed in a large metal watertight box. Boutan also devised an ingenious method of artificial lighting for underwater use: A large glass jar, mounted on top of a barrel, enclosed a lighted spirit lamp, and by means of a tube the operator could spray magnesium powder over the flame creating an intense light. The barrel housed an air supply that ensured enough oxygen for a reasonable burning time.

About five years after the publication of Boutan's book another Frenchman, E. Peau, built a metal camera housing and started taking underwater photographs. Peau was working in very murky waters, so he devised a piece of equipment that enabled him to eliminate at least some of the dirty water between the camera lens and subject. A glass cone was filled with clean water and sealed with glass discs at each end. Placed over the camera lens port, this cone extended the field of vision. It is still used for close-up work in dirt-suspended waters, for example examining defects in harbour and dam walls.

In 1913 J. E. Williamson designed a structure that bought him fame and fortune—the Williamson Tube. The tube itself was a simple enough device, consisting of a flexible shaft, about 3 feet or 1 metre in diameter, at the bottom end of which was built a steel observation sphere. Through the glass ports of this sphere Williamson filmed the underwater world as the public had never before seen it— factually. Williamson made several highly successful underwater films, including the original *Twenty Thousand Leagues Under the Sea*.

A Dr. W. H. Longley was probably the first to attempt underwater photography in colour. Longley developed his heavy brass underwater camera housing in 1917. A few years later, in 1923, he produced colour photographs of underwater scenes by natural light.

Approaching 1930, scientists were taking an interest in underwater photography in appreciable numbers: William Beebe, with his famous bathysphere; Dr. C. H. Martin; Dr. W. Schmitt; Sir Robert H. Davis—all made their contributions. About this time E. R. Fenimore Johnson started to manufacture underwater photographic equipment, and the company was later to become the largest of its kind in the world.

The year 1943 saw the invention of the Cousteau-Gagnan aqualung. Although this apparatus was in no way photographic, it opened up a new freedom for the underwater swimmer, and more important, a potential market for underwater photographic equipment.

From here on the picture is more familiar. Cousteau produced *The Silent World* and many other films. Hans Hass completed several books and films, and now we even have regular underwater features on television. Progress, considering the excellent start given by Dr. Boutan, was slow at first, but the latter years have seen great advances in this relatively new photographic field.

Choosing the camera

The selection of the camera you intend to take under water depends upon a permutation of requirements; whether you want to take still photographs or cine, whether the equipment will be used for purely amateur purposes or whether you intend to cash in on possible commercial aspects, whether you wish to concentrate on colour or black-and-white, and whether you need flash or other artificial light forms.

If we begin with the selection of a still camera, we come across a further sub-division; standard cameras that are enclosed in waterproof housings, and underwater cameras that are built for this purpose and have watertight seals as an integral part of their manufacture. Let us first discuss the most popular standard cameras that can be quickly converted by placing them in an appropriate housing.

Starting with the elimination of cameras that for most practical purposes are too difficult to accommodate in an enclosure, we can cross off our list cameras with bellows and cameras that use glass plates or sheet (cut) film. This guides us to cameras that are compact in design and use film in rolls. Desirable features would include: A minimum number of twelve exposures on each roll of film (you don't want to keep bobbing to the surface to re-load); and integral film-wind and shutter-cocking knob or lever (this eliminates one control shaft); and provision for inter-

changing lenses (not underwater). This permutation seems
to indicate a 35 mm camera, and in fact this type is the most
popular. The average 35 mm with interchangeable lenses is
a compact instrument taking 36 exposures, and an underwater housing can easily be made for it. There are also a
range of ready-made housings to fit specific cameras.

Cameras with a larger negative format taking twelve
pictures $2\frac{1}{4}$ inches (6 cm by 6 cm) square on 120 film,
would seem to suffer by comparison. The camera shape is
larger and costs, both initially and running, are consider-
ably greater, but if your approach is purely professional,
the larger negative can give better saleable quality—
particularly with colour transparencies. Underwater photographs, however, due to their comparative rarity, do not
suffer from this problem to the same extent as photographs
taken on land.

If price is the main consideration, then a box-type camera
in a simple housing can prove useful if its limitations are
realized. The fixed shutter speed of a box camera, around
1/50th of a second, is adequate from the point of exposure
if the subject is not moving, but the small aperture, at
about F 11, curtails exposure severely. This means that a
reasonably fast film should be used for its wide exposure
latitude—quality is not a prime consideration because it
can't be obtained. Also, the fixed-focus lens will render
anything nearer than 8 feet or 2.5 metres distinctly blurred;
and the underwater visibility can easily be as poor as this.
It is necessary in most cases to fit the box camera with a
supplementary or portrait lens that will fix the point of
focus at about 6 feet or 2 metres.

There are a few cameras on the market that are designed
specifically for underwater use; a typical example is the
Japanese Nikonos. Sealing is obtained by the use of 'O'
rings, with a glass port on the lens to ensure that the water
does not come into contact with the surface of the lens.
Thirty-six exposures are available on 35 mm film. The
standard lens is a semi-wide angle in an interchangeable

mount, and there are other lenses available. Range-finders are dispensed with—they are almost impossible to use under water anyway—focussing being carried out by scale. A range of accessories (close-up lenses, flash guns) is also available.

This type of camera has other applications. It can be used on land in driving rain, or when water ski-ing or boating. The seals ensure that it is also dust-proof, which is useful in certain climates.

Selecting cine cameras poses similar problems. For example the 'old fashioned' double run standard 8 mm film uses a 25 ft (7·6 m) length of film that is exposed along one side for about 2 minutes 5 seconds, then it is reversed (which means getting out of the water) and a further run of the same time is made; and 2 minutes isn't really much time to film under water. If you require 8 mm film ensure you get a camera that uses runs of at least 100 ft (30 m), whether it is standard 8, super 8 or whatever. This will ensure a run of at least 8 minutes 20 seconds before you have to surface.

16 mm cameras take spools of either 50 or 100 ft—sometimes more. A model taking 100 ft is obviously better than the one taking less.

By virtue of the continuous movement, steady exposure is essential in cine, and a coupled automatic exposure meter becomes almost a necessity—certainly a most desirable extra. The same can be said of electric drive, because this eliminates the need for a winding control apart from making long sequences possible. Cine cameras made specifically for underwater use are rare and expensive; usually a waterproof housing has to be purchased, or made, to fit a particular standard camera.

8 mm cameras are adequate for most amateur purposes, but if you fancy trying to make a profit from your filming—submitting to television for example—then you will have to use 16 mm at least, and a shutter speed of 24 frames per second as against the usual 16 f.p.s. But before you decide

to speculate, find out the price of 16 mm and 35 mm cine film. You might change your mind!

Choosing the lens

Selecting the most suitable lens for the job is just as important under water as it is above, probably even more so, because on land it is a simple matter to change lenses if you are not satisfied with a specific focal length, whereas the underwater photographer is stuck with the lens he submerges with.

The most important point in the selection of a lens for underwater use is the fact that particles suspended in the water form, in varying degrees, a floating barrier between lens and subject, reducing visibility and degrading the image in the same way as a fog or mist. Added to this is the disadvantage that the lens, peering through its protective glass or plastic port, sees objects in the same way as the eye does when looking through a mask; that is, everything seems nearer, and consequently larger. This has the effect of increasing the effective focal length of the lens (a standard lens under water will function as a semi-telephoto). Now, photographic visibility under water will often be no more than 33 ft or 10 m, and some photographers have to work with visibility no more than 6 ft or 2 m. This means that the photographer has to utilize his limited area of vision to the utmost advantage by including additional areas around the normal field of view—a close-up horizon technique— with a wide angle lens. Thus it is obvious that the magnifying effect of water, turning a standard lens into a semi-telephoto, is a step in the wrong direction.

In addition to increasing the area of photographable visibility, a wide angle lens enables the photographer to move in closer to the subject. This means that there will be less water and suspended sediment between the lens and subject, resulting in a sharper image.

Because all lenses suffer an apparent increase in focal

length when used under water, a semi-wide angle really becomes the equivalent of a standard lens, so it is advisable, particularly in waters of low visibility, to use a full wide angle lens. (If cost prohibits this, a semi-wide angle will still prove adequate for a lot of work). In fact a lot of good work has been produced in low visibility water with standard lenses, particularly with close-ups. So do not let the lack of a more suitable lens prevent you taking your camera under water. The table shown here will serve as a guide if your camera possesses the facility to interchange lenses.

The maximum aperture (the light-gathering potential) of a lens is an item that has to be related to cost. The wider the aperture the more expensive the optic, particularly in the wide angle field. Although the ability of the wide aperture lens to produce results under poor lighting conditions is an obvious advantage, the introduction of modern films, both colour and black-and-white, makes this facility less of an advantage than it was. If money is spent on additional optical equipment it is better, in my opinion, to go for wider angle than wider *aperture*. In general a wide angle lens with an aperture of around f/3·5 will prove quite adequate.

Camera	Standard Lens	Semi-Wide Angle	Full Wide Angle
Still 35 mm.	50 mm.	35 mm.	25–28 mm
Still 2¼ × 2¼	80 mm.	65 mm.	40–45 m
Cine 8 mm.	12·5 mm.	8–10 mm.	6·6 m
Cine 16 mm.	26 mm.	18 mm.	10–14

Housings

If an ordinary camera is to be used under be necessary to house it in a water an

F

enclosure. Only a few years ago the enthusiast had to build his own housing, or have one made, but the growth of underwater swimming has been such that commercial housings for a wide range of cameras are available. In addition there are specialist firms who will tailor a housing for almost any camera. In between the two extremes of doing-it-yourself or purchasing a manufactured article lies a third, hybrid method; a clear plastic box of suitable dimensions is supplied, complete with sealing lid, gasket and control rods. This only entails fitting the camera so that it is secure in the box, then drilling holes and fitting the control rods. It is a cheaper method than the other two, but you have to be reasonably proficient with a drill.

The selection, or construction, of an underwater camera housing depends, apart from the camera body, on the focal length of the lens and the number of controls that are required. A housing that has an inadequate port or lens window can cause severe cut-off on the negative if a wide angle lens is used, while excessive controls require more holes drilled in the housing, creating additional area of potential leakage and adding to the difficulty of construction.

The suitability of a wide lens is a simple matter; just fit the lens and take a picture, you can then check the negative for cut-off. More complex is the problem of which controls to dispense with. Some are obviously essential, but the order of importance between focus, shutter speed and aperture causes a lot of argument if one or two need to be omitted. If the aperture control were left out, this would necessitate leaving the lens aperture wide open to ensure that the shutter speeds could obtain the maximum variety of exposure. The consequent loss in depth of field and the difficulty of focusing by scale makes this undesirable. Having (on paper at least) obtained aperture preference over shutter speed, we are left with aperture v. focus. Personally, I have found that if the focus control is omitted and the focusing scale pre-set at, say 6 ft or 2 m, it is usually possible

to swim into focus; but if the aperture control is omitted it is impossible to obtain correct exposure if the lighting changes. In other words, you can swim into focus but you can't swim into correct exposure. Here, then, is an arbitrary list of controls in their order of preference:

(a) Shutter release
(b) Film wind-on and shutter cock or (in cine) motor wind
(c) Aperture setting
(d) Focus
(e) Shutter speed

Of course some cameras do not have an integral film wind and shutter cocking knob or lever, but this is true of the average.

Film, filters and development

The amateur underwater cine photographer will rarely have the equipment to develop his own film, and will rely on the correct filter-exposure combination for the best effect. However the still photographer is well advised to buy a daylight developing tank and do his own developing (of the negative, not necessarily the print), particularly for black-and-white film. It is quite easy, cheaper, and allows tremendous flexibility of the scale of tones and contrast of the negative or transparency.

There are various methods employed for black-and-white film. One is to load the camera with slow or medium speed film, expose at double the rated speed (or even treble), and then develop for around 50% longer than the recommended time. This has the effect of increasing the contrast, which is good because underwater scenes are lacking in this respect. It also means that you are using a faster shutter speed and smaller aperture, which will help to give sharper prints. Although this method produces pictures that are probably better for publication, and seem to be preferred by the average viewer, the result is not an accurate interpretation of the scene viewed.

To make a really accurate record of your dives we have to use the technique of the land-based photographer when recording misty scenes. Like a surface mist or fog, the underwater world is composed of thousands of delicate half-tones, there are no rich blacks, although sparkling highlights occur when, for example, a shaft of light strikes ascending bubbles. Getting a full range of half-tones on print means using a fast film, normal exposure, and normal or less than normal developing times. Alternatively you can use a medium speed film, over-expose slightly, and curtail development by about 10%. The first method provides the widest tonal variation, and the latter a finer grain structure.

Before arriving at any of the above mentioned methods, it is useful to start your technique at the half-way mark, and to develop modifications as you see the results. For your first attempts in black-and-white, load your camera with medium speed film e.g. Plus-X, F.P.4., expose at a speed rated 50% higher than that stated on the packet or carton, and increase development by 20%. You can then adjust the combination if the final prints displease you.

Whether to use a filter with black-and-white film is open to discussion. A light yellow filter can increase contrast slightly, but the end result is a matter of personal taste, and you have to try both methods before you reach any conclusion. A filter requires an increase in exposure, owing to the decrease in light transmission that it causes.

It is not intended to go into details about the various types and makes of colour film, but a few fundamentals must be explained if the colour photographer—in cine or still—is not to grope blindly, wasting both time and money.

The most important aspect of underwater photography is the fact that water has a filtering effect on colours, at the red end of the spectrum in particular. In practice this means that red, orange, and yellow gradually disappear with increasing depth; at only 33 ft or 10 m, red has vanished, and a little deeper down the whole scene will be recorded a monotonous blue-grey. There are, however, two ways of restoring the colour balance; artificial lighting in the form of flash or continuous flood will replace colours at their surface intensity at any depth, but a more natural effect can be obtained by using a colour filter of the appropriate density to correct the balance, although this procedure is only effective down to a depth of 33 ft or 10 m. Suitable filters are manufactured by Kodak, and are known as 'colour-correcting red', or CC-R. They are available in a range of densities and the following table—an unscientific one I have evolved from personal experience—can be used as a guide.

Depth	Filter suggested	Increase in exposure
5 feet or 1·5 metres	CC-10-R	30%
10 feet or 3 metres	CC-30-R	80%
20 feet or 6 metres	CC-50-R	150%
30 feet or 9 metres	As dense as possible, try two CC-50-R	300%?

The trouble is, you do not always swim on a level plane, and it is difficult to change filters under water. If you are stuck with the filter you fit on the surface, a good all-rounder is the CC-40-R. One thing remains to be pointed out; the increase in exposure suggested is purely arbitrary and the colour correction, at best, will only be approximate.

Lighting and exposure

For still photography, a flash gun using expendable bulbs can, with modifications, be used under water—only the condenser, battery and camera lead need waterproofing; the bulb socket can be in contact with the water because an electrical circuit always takes the path of least resistance. The bulbs are fitted and removed in exactly the same way as on land.

The correct exposure calculations, when using flash bulbs under water, can only be arrived at by trial and error with that particular flash gun. Use the bulb manufacturer's guide numbers, then adjust the figure, if necessary, after studying the results.

Flash guns for use under water are manufactured to fit specific underwater cameras such as the Nikonos. On the other hand, a flash gun can be specially made for the purpose. Most underwater magazines (there is a list at the back of this book) contain advertisements of firms that specialize in underwater housings. One thing you must not try to improvise yourself is an underwater electronic flash gun. If you want to use electronic flash under water—and it is a valuable asset—use one made specifically for the purpose. Electronic flash guns build up a very high peak of power before they discharge, and you can't afford a leak under water.

Cine photographers have a more acute problem; flash is out of the question because cine film requires a continuous flood of light. Such equipment has to be adequately enclosed, with a powerful accumulator to compensate for the continuous drain on current, and equipment is not cheap. Something like 300 watts of lighting produces enough light for most purposes.

When using available or natural lighting, or a continuous flood unit, you will require the accuracy of an exposure meter. Several are made specially for use under water—ask your local camera shop about one.

Exposure meters should be used in the most simple manner, from the camera position, facing the subject. This method has proved successful in cameras that possess built-in automatic exposure meters. Difficult scenes, such as back-lit views, can be handled after a little experience of average conditions has been obtained.

Items to Note

Underwater photography demands methodical habits. There are so many bits and pieces that can be forgotten, and the dive ruined as a result: bags of silica gel to prevent internal misting of the housing, screws, tools, spare 'O' rings —and all this in addition to your aqualung equipment. Make a thorough list of every single item required, check it fully before you depart on a dive, and again before you leave for home.

12

Archaeology Under Water

The general area of sea bed from the shore down to about 200 feet, or 60 metres, contains the greatest amount of archaeological and historical material, and there are good reasons for this. Ancient ships, owing to a sparse knowledge of navigation chose, wherever possible, the shipping routes that hugged the coastline. Many foundered on treacherous rocks that lay just below the surface, when they would have been safer farther out; the coastline is a particularly dangerous place for vessels, especially in bad weather. Also, the level of the sea does not remain constant through the ages: it has moved up and down—excluding tides—throughout the ages because of periods of glaciation. When the ice ages were at their height, vast amounts of ice were locked up at the poles, and the sea dropped far below its present level. Over a period, since the end of the last ice age some 8,000 years ago, the level of the sea has been rising, with the result that many towns, cities and harbours of the past are now lying under the sea. And glaciation is not the only cause; land subsidence, earthquakes and erosion have all contributed their share. Thus the richest fields for exploration lie in the zone most accessible to the diver, and provided some training can be obtained even a comparative layman is in a position to contribute to our knowledge of the past.

Many clubs have assisted scientists and archaeologists throughout the world, and particularly in America and

Britain. In Britain these include: Investigating the cranogs (artificial islands) in Loch Lomond; Roman wells; a survey that has uncovered many items of historical interest from the Thames—for which the club received a certificate from the London Museum; the successful search for the Mary Rose, a warship that overturned and sank in the Solent in 1545; and several seaweed surveys to study the effects of pollution etc.

The roman wreck at Pudding Pan Rock

Pudding Pan Rock is a shoal in the Thames estuary, about 4 miles north of Whitstable, Kent, England. The name derives from the large quantity of pottery that has, in the past, been dredged up by the nets of local fishermen. The first finds were, indeed, very suitable for cooking puddings— as the fishermens' wives were quick to note—although later plates of various shapes and sizes, some plain and others with a simple embossed motif, were brought up.

The pottery is classed as Samian ware, and was made in central France in the second century A.D. The main production centre during this period was Lezoux, from where the pottery probably came, being transported by river to the coast of Gaul, and from there to London, a destination it nearly never reached. The British Museum, in Great Russell Street, now houses a collection from this very consignment; so it did reach its destination—a trifle late! The ware is stamped with the maker's name, Satvrini.

Several expeditions, both helmet and aqualung diving, have failed to locate what might be left of the wreck. Situated where it is, near the mouth of the Thames, care has to be taken with tides, and although visibility, at its best, might reach as far as 8 feet or 2½ metres, it will probably be in the region of inches or centimetres. Future expeditions will find the diving dull and uninspiring. There is even the point that there might never have been a wreck—there might be some other reason for this accumulation of Samian ware. Still, Pudding Pan Rock has, at the time of writing, the nearest possibility of being the site of a Roman wreck in British coastal water, because none has ever been found.

Lost towns and harbours

The story of Ravenser Odd illustrates just one aspect of reclamation by the sea.

Spurn Head lies at the mouth of the River Humber, a curling headland in the shape of a crook, one side facing the river and very susceptible to silting up. At the beginning of the thirteenth century, marine deposits built up a small sand bank on the inside of the Head. At first, local fishermen used the sand bank for laying out catches and equipment, but as the exposed land became more stable, commerce moved in and Ravenser Odd was born. At its peak, the town was a threat to its neighbour, Grimsby, and even had a Member of Parliament. Then, the forces that formed its foundation started to reverse the process; by the end of the fourteenth century, Ravenser Odd had disappeared. The actual site is still in dispute, but Ravenser Odd was, for a while, a very real place. Now it is covered by the waters of the Humber, or possibly the North Sea.

At 11 a.m. of the 7th June, 1692, Port Royal, Jamaica, was a thriving if nefarious town. By mid-day, an earthquake had reduced two-thirds of the town to below sea level. The death toll was around two thousand. Nearly two hundred and fifty years later, in 1959, an American, Edwin Link, led an underwater archaeological expedition that recovered a wealth of artifacts and surveyed the remains of the sunken site, giving historians a wealth of material with which to reconstruct an important period of our past.

The list is endless. When the New World was being explored, boats tended to follow routes dictated by the Atlantic currents. Historians have charted these routes, and study has revealed the sites of many wrecks from this period.

In the Mediterranean, there are over sixty known submerged cities and harbours of the past. Among them are Helike, Apollonia, and the Great Harbour of Pharos. Fewer than a dozen have been surveyed by diving archaeologists and not one, at the time of writing, thoroughly.

Preservation of iron and wood

Techniques and equipment have evolved to the stage where amateur diving groups are capable of lifting, and removing, comparatively heavy objects from the bottom of the sea bed. This leads to the danger of untutored enthusiasts removing artifacts without ensuring that the correct treatment for preservation of the objects is available. Iron and wood, after a long immersion in sea water, will disintegrate rapidly on exposure to air. However, there are occasions— such as difficulty in re-locating the site—when immediate removal might be advisable. For these occasions the following notes might be of help. Many valuable finds are lost every year because of incorrect treatment after recovery.

In the case of iron, the chemical treatment will necessitate removal of the oxygen that has formed at the surface of the metal. Marine encrustations also form on the surface. These can be removed by gentle tapping with a hammer while the object is immersed in a bath or other water-filled container. If the iron is delicate or extremely important— such as a rare cannon—the removal and preservation is best left to an expert. However, it is important that the whole object is kept damp and away from direct contact with air. If a large enough container is not available, the parts should be covered with wet material such as sacking, and further covered with plastic sheet until a suitable receptacle is obtained. While immersed in water the iron will keep until you can bring in an expert. Don't try to 'improvise' methods of drying; the correct process takes many months, and trying to shorten this time could lead to the loss of the item. Brass requires no treatment, just tap the growths off with a hammer, rinse, then polish.

Wood, in fresh water, has an indefinite life, but in most sea water it is susceptible to attack by shipworm. This organism can eliminate a sturdy wooden pile in a few short years. Some woods—probably by luck, such as having been buried in silt, or various oils in them—will resist the ravage of shipworm for long periods, sometimes centuries, and in such cases attempts at preservation are directed towards removing the moisture in the wood without drying it (this would cause its destruction) and replacing the moisture with paraffin (the wax, not the oil) or some other substance. The wood, having been immersed in fresh water for a specific period, is removed from the water and is placed in a container along with alcohol, or initially water and alcohol. In the latter case a series of changes gradually produces a 100% alcohol solution. When the wood has been immersed in alcohol for several weeks the alcohol is replaced by xylene and left for a week or more. The xylene is then renewed, and slivers of paraffin wax added until a well-saturated solution is obtained. The wood is left in this solution for several weeks before being removed. When the treatment is complete the excess wax coating is removed by polishing gently.

It must be pointed out that this process can only be used with safety on wood that has been retrieved from fresh water. The results are very unpredictable on wood that has been immersed in sea water. The reason for this is probably the presence of salt; therefore it is essential that sea water saturated wood is soaked in fresh water, with frequent changes, for as long a period as possible before commencing the alcohol bath.

This process can also be used to preserve leather and bone.

13

Biology Under Water

There are still vast areas of land that are biologically un-
surveyed, even after centuries of exploration and scientific
advance. Imagine, then, the problem that lies in studying a
far larger area, the underwater world, from scratch, without the benefit of accumulated years of exploration. For
many years to come the trained diver will be of immense
use to the scientists beginning to tackle this mammoth task
(provided, of course, that in addition to his diving ability
he has some knowledge of the science he is assisting). It is to
be hoped that education authorities will bring underwater
sciences into the curriculum of many classes of further
education for the amateur archaeologist/biologist diver.

It is not possible, in this book, to give even a firm outline
of underwater biology. As in the section on archaeology, a
few examples followed by hints on preservation and treatment are all I can provide.

The layman and underwater research

Many diving clubs have assisted museums in surveys. For
example The Westminster branch of the BSAC has assisted
National Museum of Wales on a botanical study of some
lakes in the Snowdon area of north Wales. There were no
botanists in the group; specimens found were sent to the
Museum for identification. By obtaining details such as the
maximum depths at which plants grow, and their general

distribution; temperatures at intervals down to the bottom; type of bottom; visibility at all depths etc., the club built up a set of data sheets that added to the knowledge of natural history of these lakes, in which so little exploration has been done. As the identification of species is done by an expert, the divers can get on with the aspect of underwater research in which the enthusiastic layman can compete with a professor on level terms—accurate recording.

Lakes, in any country, are rich in legend, and north Wales is no exception. A 'sunken city' lies at the bottom of Lake Bala, and a 'monster' at the bottom of Glaslyn—at the bottom because the monster was killed before being deposited in the freezing water. Thus, while providing good areas for the more tangible practice of botanical exploration, every mound on the lake bottom is liable to titillate the imagination.

At sea, liason between diver and scientist is increasing. Clubs have assisted museums and universities in collecting everything from Mediterranean Gobies (an attractive little fish, one species of which—*Mistichthys luzonensis*—can lay a double claim to fame; it is the smallest known fish, and also the smallest known vertebrate) to seaweed, the latter particularly for pollution evaluation.

But don't, repeat don't, volunteer for work such as this unless you are sure that you possess the discipline to record with painstaking accuracy. Even 'failure' can provide useful information; if a search for a specific fish or plant proves negative, its recorded absence could fit in a little part of the natural history jig-saw.

Collecting and preservation

Collecting aquatic specimens, both flora and fauna, for the sake of a memento, is to be discouraged. For a record of your dive a photograph is a better medium. However, all divers can cultivate an active interest in natural history under water. Fish—even outside the frying pan—can be interesting subjects, and this will often entail collecting specific specimens and treating them for further study. It must be stressed that these preservation hints are for general use by the diver collecting on his own behalf; when collecting for an authority such as a museum, the exact preservation procedure for a specific item will be given. Specimens, even of a similar species, may require slightly different treatment according to the requirements of the study.

Coral: A long soak (minimum one week) in fresh water with frequent changes of water to remove the salt—and that's all. The coral is then left to dry out *slowly*. Some corals, such as gorgonia, tend to lose their colour after exposure to light, and this can only be rectified by re-soaking in a dye of the same colour.

Fish: The animal should be alive for the best results. The fish should first be doped, otherwise the muscles will contract on fixing (and in any case the doping is more humane). This is achieved by placing the fish in fresh water (for fresh water fish, use distilled water). When you can pick the creature up without it moving, it should be ready. It can then be killed by dropping it into a solution of 70% ethyl alcohol and 30% water. The body is then injected with a 10% formalin solution, and preserved in the same liquid. In the case of marine fish, make up the 10% formalin solution with sea water. Formalin can be obtained from a chemist or drug store, and the 10% solution is made up by mixing one part formalin with nine parts water.

Plants: Two methods are offered for preserving seaweed, the one chosen depending on how much time and patience you have. The second method is the best for display. (1) Soak the plant in fresh water for six hours, changing the water several times. Drain off thoroughly, and soak in glycerine for at least eighteen hours. Drain again, lay the plant on a good quality unglazed (not shiny) paper, and dry in a warm, dry room. (2) Collect and keep the plants in fresh water until ready for treatment. When ready, drain the plant and arrange on a sheet of good quality unglazed paper. Place paper and plant on another sheet of unglazed paper and cover with washed butter-muslin. On top of the muslin place another sheet of the paper. This procedure is repeated until a pile of plants interspaced with paper and muslin is obtained. The pile is placed between two sheets of board—hardboard is perfectly suitable—and gentle pressure applied, e.g. a flower press. The papers should be changed every day for three days; the specimens should be ready in about seven or eight days. When dry, the muslin should be peeled off carefully, and the specimens should adhere to the paper, ready for display or observation. Where the plant does not stick to the paper, a touch of glue such as clear contact adhesive, might be needed.

Sea urchins: If only the shell is needed, cut carefully round the 'foot' and remove the innards with your finger. The urchin is then placed in a saucepan of water (the smell is horrible) and brought to the boil. The spines can then be scraped off with a knife, but be careful because the shell is very delicate. A few drops of household bleach added to the final water will make the colours of the shell more vivid. If the specimen is desired with the spines intact, and this is far more natural, remove the innards as before, wash out well in several changes of fresh water, and either soaked in a 10% formalin solution or dried thoroughly in a gentle oven with the door open. Again, the latter solution smells awful.

Starfish: Starfish should be doped in fresh water as for fish. After several hours in the fresh water it can be fixed in a 10% formalin solution. When removed from the solution, the starfish is tied down to a board and thoroughly dried. If not tied down while drying, the starfish will tend to curl up.

14

Spearfishing

The arguments for and against spearfishing have caused more heated discussion than in any other water sport. Despite this, as a sport it is still popular in some parts of the world. Possibly, in time, the camera will replace the spear—as it has the rifle on land to a large extent—although photography under water is much more difficult than on land, and the cheapest underwater photographic apparatus is far more expensive than its spearfishing counterpart, the hand spear.

It has been suggested that this method of fishing is denuding the sea of its fish life, even though rod and line anglers, by sheer weight of numbers, probably remove a greater number of fish from the sea in a day than spearfishermen do in a week. And there has never been any suggestion that the rod and reel would deplete our waters. However, I must place on record that I am against competitive spearfishing, although I have no objection whatsoever in spearing fish for food. Indeed, if you are diving in a remote site this is probably the only way to ensure a supply of fresh food.

Spearfishing correctly practiced is carried out using fins, mask snorkel, spear or harpoon—and a deep breath. Aqualung apparatus is frowned on as unsporting, and has in fact been made illegal in some countries.

Men have, for hundreds of years, utilized a spear or like instrument for the purpose of catching fish. But it is only since the introduction of the mask and fins, giving man visibility and propulsion under water, that he has competed against the fish on more favourable terms. Even so, the most competitive fanatic would agree that to spear a friendly, inedible fish is more than just unsporting—it is wanton destruction. It is therefore important to be able to recognize not only those fish most suitable for the pot, but also the inedible variety, whose death would benefit nobody.

Equipment

Essential equipment for spearfishing consists of fins, mask and spear; but of almost equal necessity is a snorkel and, in some waters, some form of protective clothing. If you use protective clothing you will also require a weight belt to correct buoyancy, and a lifejacket for safety's sake. A knife is no luxury; in fact, considering the amount of tough line that the spearfisherman could get entangled with, it can be considered an essential. Let us start with the various types of spear and harpoon, and their capabilities.

The simplest underwater hunting implement, and one requiring a great deal of patience and skill, is the hand spear. This is a shaft of varying length, manufactured from wood, metal or fibreglass, with a sharp steel spear head, usually interchangeable. The velocity, or thrust, of the hand spear is usually improved by the addition to a loop of elastic on the end opposite the head turning it, in effect, into a hand-sling spear.

When hunting with a hand spear, patience is required because of its limited range. An above average knowledge of the underwater world is required when fish have to be approached closely and some fish, such as the poisonous weever, the sting ray, and the congers and morays, are best avoided altogether.

Despite—or perhaps because of—the above comments, many skilled spearfishermen insist that hunting with the hand spear gives the most equal sporting conditions in man's contest with the fish. Certainly, many fish weighing over 50 pounds or 23 kilograms have been recorded as having been caught with this primitive instrument; ample proof of the degree of skill that can be reached.

Hand spears have been produced in lengths exceeding 10 feet or 3 metres, but it must be pointed out that in some water visibility is often less than that, and it is rather pointless looking for prey when you can't even see the end of your spear. In any case a good all-round length for a hand spear is around 4 feet or 1·5 metres.

Most underwater hunting is carried out with a spear gun. This instrument can be divided into three types according to the method of propelling the harpoon or spear: rubber strands, coil springs, and compressed gas.

The most popular spear gun is the type powered by rubber strands, and this works on the same principle as that of the catapult or ancient cross-bow, although some models increase the power by adding additional elastic strands.

Although powerful, rubber strand powered guns are the cheapest to buy owing to the simplicity of construction. The price, no doubt, accounts for much of their popularity, while their very simplicity renders them less liable to mechanical failure—and they are easier to repair when they do fail. They are usually the easiest of the three types of gun to load.

Of possible danger to the operator—as with a catapult— is the possibility of a strand snapping while under stress or being cocked. Spare strands are relatively inexpensive, but those in use should be checked regularly for faults or signs of wear. Even if nothing suspicious is seen, it is a good plan to replace the strands at frequent intervals.

The next gun, in order of popularity and price, is that using a coil spring as the power source. Coil spring guns are usually of more robust construction than their rubber strand cousins, and the increased difficulty of manufacture is reflected in the price. This type of gun has a more streamlined appearance than the rubber strand model, and the position of the handle, in the middle of the barrel, gives a better balance.

Coil springs lose their efficiency and power with use, and the spring can break, but this presents the operator with no danger, only inconvenience. The springs can usually be replaced quite easily. Ensure that no sand gets into the spring or any other moving parts, and also that you oil the metal mechanical parts before and after use.

The 'big daddy' of the spearfishing world is the compressed gun, which is immensely powerful and easy to load. Air is pumped into a chamber and retained by a piston inside the barrel, which prevents the compressed air from escaping, and the gun can be fired and re-loaded many times without further pumping. Charging pumps are usually included in the purchase price.

Compressed air guns are virtually silent in operation under water. They are used by the majority of spearfishermen in competition.

Should a harpoon not prove immediately fatal, or even miss the target altogether, it can easily get lost. All harpoons are secured to the gun by a length of nylon line. The line is fed out by a reel or clip attached to the gun, which makes the recovery of the harpoon a simple matter.

The barbed head of the harpoon should be interchangeable, because no particular head is best for all types of fish. It is unlikely that, on an average hunt, you would have the correct head fitted for all the fish you meet, so should you be hunting for a particular fish the right head should be fitted.

The trident head, which can have two prongs or more, is often the most suitable for flat fish, small fish and most bottom fish. Usually, trident prongs and barbs are fashioned from soft steel, which makes them easier to keep sharp and straighten, should they bend.

Larger fish require a heavier spear head, which is usually a single point, with one or more pivoted levers that prevent the harpoon from being pulled out too easily.

While on the subject of spear guns, remember that they are designed to kill, and even the smallest type is capable of killing a human being. So here are a few rules that should always be adhered to, not just most of the time but *always*:

1 **Never point a gun, loaded or unloaded, at anyone.**

2 **Never carry a loaded gun on land; a gun should always be loaded or unloaded in the water.**

3 **Never hunt in the vicinity of other people, whether bathers, divers, fishermen or yachtsmen.**

4 **Never fire a gun towards the surface.**

5 **Always use the safety catch, but never rely on it.**

6 **Never leave equipment, particularly harpoon heads, around on a beach.**

7 **Under water, never let your gun dangle, keep it held correctly.**

Should someone accidentally get transfixed by a harpoon. remember that its job is to hold tight, so do not try to pull it out. Call for a doctor, or get the patient to one, as soon as possible.

There are various gun licence and firearms acts in force around the world, and some of these statuary regulations might or might not apply to spear guns. It is best to consult your local police for a ruling on this subject, because regulations vary so much.

Of immense value to a spearfisherman, if no boat cover is available, is a good float with a form of keep-net attached. This can be fashioned quite cheaply by blowing up a car tyre inner tube and using waterproof contact adhesive to glue netting, or cloth, over one open side. The float is used covered side down, and the receptacle provided can be used to hold catches, or equipment, while the tyre itself can support a spearfisherman taking a breather. One point; a float of any kind will scud across the water very quickly in a good breeze or current, and can vanish in no time. So ensure that the float or raft is fitted with a line attached to some form of bottom anchor.

Training

Once you have obtained your equipment you will, no doubt, desire to get under water and bag a big 'un. But wait. If a thing is worth doing, it's worth doing well. A little advance planning and some training will make you more competent, insuring against some frustrating experiences when you finally go hunting.

Spearfishing is an exacting, exhausting occupation. When you sight your fish you have to get down quickly to dispatch him. The spearfisherman descends, and ascends, at a much greater speed than the aqualung diver; pressures change swiftly, and the ears have to be cleared with machine-gun rapidity—as against the leisurely pace of the aqualung diver—causing greater stresses on ears and sinuses. Also, the spearfisherman hunts using his own lungs as his sole air supply. So it is easy to see that the first training essential is to get in good physical trim. When in the pool, do plenty of lengths and practice a clean, splashless surface dive. After all, the fish are more used to the water than you are, and you are training to get on more equal terms.

The principles of swimming with fins, mask and snorkel are laid out in Chapter 2. While brushing-up on this, also read (you should already have done so) the physical and medical aspects on Chapter 3, paying particular attention to Exhaustion, Ears and Sinus, and Anoxia. The last-named is probably the greatest spearfishing hazard (apart from a short-sighted hunter without his safety catch on) because of the amount of breath-holding carried out. DON'T practice hyperventilation—before you dive, only a couple of deep breaths are necessary—and on surfacing, recover fully before the next dive. When practising in the pool, do not fight to hold your breath while under water; the secret is to relax—try thinking about something else. But don't forget to recover fully between each dive, and forget trying to set up breath-holding records. Your job is to get down, spear your fish and surface; if you want to spend time looking around then use an aqualung.

The first few shots with your gun will soon prove that you need a little practice. If you have access to the sea, obtain a float and hang your practice target (a piece of weighted wood or similar material) from it with a 10 foot or 3 metre length of line. In a swell, or with choppy water, the float will ride up and down, making the target jump about. This motion is not usually present in still waters such as pools and lakes, but you can still get some practice in. This method can, of course, be reversed or inverted; the line is tied to a weight on the bottom, and the wooden target is not weighted, allowing to float, but be careful not to have the line too short or you will stir up the bottom sediment.

There are many books on the subject of fish haunts and recognition. These are written mainly for the rod and line fisherman, but most of the contents contain valuable reference material. On the subject of recognition, don't overlook the fishmonger's slab; sometimes the fish are arranged whole, with tickets displaying the name, and a lot can be learned browsing around the shop with a good reference book (but don't forget to buy some fish once in a while to stop the fishmonger being annoyed).

The hunt

The first problem, naturally, is where to fish. Every stretch of coastline supports varying amounts of fish life, according to conditions and physical structure. Also, the better spearfisherman, by virtue of experience or knowledge, knows his fish. It is of little use looking for conger or moray along a sandy bottom—or flatfish among rock and weed.

Usually an area will be pre-destined by holidays or accessibility. In this case the reference books, plus a little judicious enquiring among the locals, are required.

The more prolific sites are often found around irregularities of the sea bed e.g. rock formations, wrecks, reefs and gullies. Dense plant life will also usually be heavily inhabited.

A clumsy, threshing dive will frighten off most fish; this is why you should practice a clean, splash-free surface dive which will slide you under the water with a minimum of disturbance. Some divers prefer to submerge by raising the top of the torso out of the water and dropping feet first, but with this method your eyes are taken off your quarry for a second, and in this time it could easily vanish.

If possible, dive from a position with the sun behind you. When the fish is within range, manoeuvre into a broadside position and aim for the area just behind the eyes. The belly area is too soft and the backbone—should you approach from above—can be too tough, especially for the hand spear.

Should the spear head impale the fish but not prove immediately fatal, don't let the poor creature struggle, wounded and possibly in pain. Grasp it firmly by the back and use your knife to sever the spinal cord just behind the head—unless the victim is a conger or moray, in which case leave it alone.

Most fish are not easily caught, or even seen. The successful spearfisherman does not rush things; he will search every rock, every hole, and every crop of weed. Acute observation is even more necessary in the case of flatfish. They usually lie on a sandy bottom, and blend with the background so well that only a close look will spot them.

There is one type of underwater creature that is neither speared nor knifed—the shellfish Crabs and lobsters and crays are caught by hand. Average or smaller specimens are held across the back, but larger animals require two hands, each hand round a claw in the case of crab or lobster.

Virtually every country has legislation prohibiting the taking of shellfish in some form or other, or various species. Quite often small crabs or lobster are prohibited, and either or both when in spawn (this is termed 'berried' and can easily be checked by looking at the underside, when the berries can easily be seen). But whether illegal or not, it is clearly crazy to take small or berried shellfish, for obvious reasons.

Appendix A

Decompression Tables

Introduction

Every diver should become acquainted with metricated decompression tables, which is why the first tables shown below are metricated. Clubs should encourage their members to use these new units. However, it is recognized that some divers currently practising decompression diving under the old measurements may find some difficulty in effecting a smooth transition, and for this reason the metricated tables are followed by tables in the old units.

Note: **All decompression tables contain a margin of error, and the human body is so variable that decompression sickness can sometimes follow even when the tables have been adhered to. So ensure that whenever decompression diving is taking place, a decompression chamber is within a few hours drive —and operative.**

DECOMPRESSION

Second and subsequent dives within 12 hours

A diver carrying out a dive on Table 1 above the limiting line, may carry out a second and subsequent dives to depths not greater than 9 m, without time restriction or further decompression. If, however, he is required to dive again to a depth exceeding 9 m within 4 hours of a previous dive to 9 m or less, or within 12 hours of a previous dive to more than 9 m, he may do so only if he is given the stops for a combined dive. A diver who has carried out a dive below the limiting line is not to carry out a further dive within 12 hours.

Stops for a combined dive

The stops for a combined dive are obtained by adding together the duration of the first and each subsequent dive to obtain a Total Time for the combined dives. This total time and the depth of the deepest dive made are used to obtain the stops in the relevant table as for a single dive. The total time of the combined dives, except that dives carried out using pure oxygen should not be considered for calculation of a combined dive, is to be limited so that the Total Time for Decompression (column 4 or 6 as applicable to the table in use) does not exceed 75 minutes.

Procedure after diving to 37 m or more

Any man who has carried out a dive to a depth of 35 m or more for a period above the limiting line in Table 1, is to remain within 4 hours travelling time of a compression chamber for 12 hours after completing the dive.

Any man who has carried out a dive of 35 m or more for a period below the limiting line in Table 1 must remain in the immediate vicinity (i.e. on board) of a compression chamber for a period of 4 hours after completing the dive, and within 4 hours travelling time of a chamber for a further 12 hours.

Terms used and methods available

1   Definition of terms

Stoppage. A calculated pause at a specific depth in the diver's ascent to allow the dispersion of excess nitrogen absorbed by the body.

Decompression. A series of stoppages and decrease in pressure to allow the diver to surface safely.

2 Methods available

The following methods of decompression are available:

Air decompression. Decompression carried out while the diver is in the water breathing air and being surfaced in accordance with Table 1.

Surface decompression. Decompression carried out in a compression chamber on the surface: with the diver breathing air and being surfaced in accordance with Table 1.

Therapeutic decompression. The recompression of a diver suffering from decompression sickness and his subsequent decompression at a slower rate than normal.

General instructions

Any diver who dives to a depth and to a period covered by the decompression tables is to carry out decompression strictly in accordance with the appropriate decompression table, except on the advice of a trained diving Medical Officer or in extreme emergency.

Maximum depth of dive

The decompression tables in this Chapter provide for a maximum dive of 61 m, but the present maximum permissible depth of dive is 55 m.

Hard work—use of decompression tables

When a diver exerts himself unduly, his body absorbs more gas than usual and he will require a longer period of decompression to eliminate this gas. *On all occasions when hard physical work is carried out by a diver, the decompression routine for the dive is to be taken as that for the next longer time increment for the dive.* Fin-swimming is rated as 'hard physical work'.

Air decompression—Table 1

Table 1 is used to obtain the times for the diver's stops in water.

Depth in metres (column 1). This column is entered with:
When breathing air, the actual deepest depth of dive.

Column 1 of Table 1 is divided into sections which contain increments of 3 m. The section used is that which immediately exceeds the depth obtained, but if there is any doubt about the accuracy of this figure, the next deeper section is to be used, e.g. if the depth obtained was 14 m and the accuracy of this depth was in doubt, the 18 m section would be used.

Duration (column 2). This is the interval of time in minutes between the time of the diver leaving the surface and the time that he leaves the bottom to commence the ascent. Where the actual duration does not coincide with one of the figures in the table, the nearest higher figure is to be taken: e.g. if the actual duration was 27 min. at 43 m, the stops would be taken for 30 min. Where there is any doubt about the accuracy of the duration, the next higher figure is to be taken and in the example quoted would be 35 min.

Limiting line. The part of each depth section above the limiting line is the ordinary working table where the risk of decompression sickness is negligible; diving for periods below the line carries a greater risk of decompression sickness and this risk increases with an increase of duration below the line. Intentional diving below the limiting line should only be undertaken when a compression chamber is immediately available on the site and then only when circumstances justify the risk.

Rate of ascent. The rate of ascent from the bottom to the first stop, between stops, and from the last stop to surface should be as near as possible (18 m per min.), a steady rate of ascent is however more important than the precise time taken to complete it. Where the diver's exhaust bubbles can be seen the correct speed of ascent is best obtained by keeping pace with the smaller bubbles.

Method of timing stops. The time for the first stop commences when the diver leaves the sea bed and the time for each subsequent stop commences when the diver leaves the preceding stop.

While every care has been taken in the compilation of these tables, neither the Ministry of Defence nor the Crown is liable for the use made of it by any person outside the service of the Ministry or the Crown, or for anything said or omitted to be said therein, or for any consequences, including any accident, or for anything done or omitted to be done as a result of the use of the tables by any such person.

TABLE 1

Metricated RN Air Decompression Tables

Reproduced with the permission of Her Majesty's Stationery Office.

(1) Depth not exceeding (metres)	(2) Duration time leaving surface to beginning of ascent not exceeding (min)	(3) Stoppages at different depths (min)					(4) Total time for decompression (min)
		15 m	12 m	9 m	6 m	3 m	
3	No limit	—	—	—	—	—	—
12	135	—	—	—	—	—	—
	165	—	—	—	—	5	5
	195	—	—	—	—	10	10
	225	—	—	—	—	15	15
	255	—	—	—	—	20	20
	330	—	—	—	—	25	25
	390	—	—	—	—	30	30
	660	—	—	—	—	35	35
	Limiting line over 660	—	—	—	—	40	40
	85	—	—	—	—	—	—
	105	—	—	—	—	5	5
	120	—	—	—	—	10	10
	135	—	—	—	—	15	15
	145	—	—	—	—	20	20

(1) Depth not exceeding (metres)	(2) Duration time leaving surface to beginning of ascent not exceeding (min)	(3) Stoppages at different depths (min)					(4) Total time for decompression (min)
		15 m	12 m	9 m	6 m	3 m	
15	160	—	—	—	—	25	25
	170	—	—	—	5	25	30
	190	—	—	—	5	30	35
	Limiting line						
	240	—	—	—	10	40	50
	360	—	—	—	30	40	70
	450	—	—	—	35	40	75
	over 450	—	—	—	35	45	80
18	60	—	—	—	—	—	—
	70	—	—	—	—	5	5
	80	—	—	—	5	5	10
	90	—	—	—	5	10	15
	100	—	—	—	5	15	20
	110	—	—	—	5	20	25
	120	—	—	—	5	25	30
	130	—	—	—	5	30	35
	Limiting line						
	140	—	—	—	10	30	40
	150	—	—	—	10	40	50
	160	—	—	—	15	40	55
	180	—	—	—	20	40	60
	200	—	—	5	30	40	75
	255	—	—	10	35	45	90
	325	—	—	20	40	45	105
	495	—	—	35	40	45	120
	over 495	—	—	35	40	50	125
21	40	—	—	—	—	5	5
	55	—	—	—	—	5	5
	60	—	—	—	5	5	10
	70	—	—	—	5	10	15
	75	—	—	—	5	15	20
	85	—	—	—	5	20	25
	90	—	—	—	5	25	30
	95	—	—	5	5	25	35
	Limiting line						
	105	—	—	5	5	35	45
	120	—	—	5	10	40	55
	135	—	—	5	20	45	70
	150	—	—	5	30	45	80
	165	—	—	10	30	50	90
	180	—	—	15	35	50	100
	210	—	—	25	40	50	115
	240	—	5	30	40	50	125
24	30	—	—	—	—	5	5
	40	—	—	—	—	5	5
	50	—	—	—	5	5	10
	55	—	—	—	5	10	15
	60	—	—	—	5	15	20
	70	—	—	—	5	20	25
	75	—	—	—	5	25	30
	Limiting line						

(1) Depth not exceeding (metres)	(2) Duration time leaving surface to beginning of ascent not exceeding (min)	(3) Stoppages at different depths (min)					(4) Total time for decompression (min)
		15 m	12m	9 m	6 m	3 m	
	80	—	—	5	5	30	40
	90	—	—	5	10	35	50
	105	—	—	5	20	40	65
	120	—	5	5	30	45	85
	140	—	5	10	35	50	100
	160	—	10	30	40	50	130
	25	—	—	—	—	—	—
	30	—	—	—	—	5	5
	40	—	—	—	5	5	10
	45	—	—	—	5	10	15
	50	—	—	—	5	15	20
	55	—	—	—	5	20	25
	60	—	—	5	5	20	30
	65	—	—	5	5	25	35
27	**Limiting line**						
	70	—	—	5	10	30	45
	75	—	—	5	15	30	50
	80	—	—	5	20	35	60
	90	—	—	5	25	40	70
	100	—	—	5	30	45	80
	110	—	5	15	35	45	100
	120	—	5	20	35	50	110
	135	5	5	25	40	50	125
	150	5	10	35	40	50	140
	20	—	—	—	—	—	—
	25	—	—	—	—	5	5
	30	—	—	—	5	5	10
	35	—	—	—	5	10	15
	40	—	—	—	5	15	20
	45	—	—	—	5	20	25
	50	—	—	5	5	20	30
	55	—	—	5	5	25	35
30	**Limiting line**						
	60	—	—	5	10	30	45
	70	—	—	5	20	35	60
	75	—	5	5	20	40	70
	80	—	5	5	20	40	80
	90	—	5	15	30	45	95
	105	—	5	25	35	50	115
	120	5	10	30	40	50	135

(1) Depth not exceeding (metres)	(2) Duration	18 m	15 m	12 m	9 m	6 m	3 m	(4) Total
	17	—	—	—	—	—	5	—
	20	—	—	—	—	—	5	5
	25	—	—	—	—	5	5	10
	30	—	—	—	—	5	10	15
	35	—	—	—	—	5	15	20
	40	—	—	—	—	5	20	25
	45	—	—	—	5	5	20	30
	Limiting line							
33	50	—	—	—	5	10	25	40
	55	—	—	—	5	15	30	50

(1) Depth not exceeding (Metres)	(2) Duration time leaving surface to beginning of ascent not exceeding (min)	(3) Stoppages at different depths (min)						(4) Total time for decompression (min)
		18 m	15 m	12 m	9 m	6 m	3 m	
	60	—	—	—	5	20	35	60
	65	—	—	5	5	20	40	70
	70	—	—	5	10	20	45	80
	75	—	—	5	15	25	45	90
	80	—	—	5	20	30	45	100
	90	—	5	5	20	40	45	115
	100	—	5	10	25	40	50	130
	110	—	5	20	30	45	50	150
	120	5	5	25	40	45	50	170
	14	—	—	—	—	—	—	—
	20	—	—	—	—	—	5	5
	25	—	—	—	—	5	5	10
	30	—	—	—	—	5	15	20
	35	—	—	—	—	5	20	25
	40	—	—	—	5	5	25	35
	Limiting line							
36	45	—	—	—	5	10	25	40
	50	—	—	—	5	15	30	50
	55	—	—	5	5	20	35	65
	60	—	—	5	10	25	40	80
	70	—	—	5	20	30	45	100
	75	—	5	5	20	35	45	110
	80	—	5	10	25	35	45	120
	90	—	5	15	30	40	50	140
	100	5	5	20	35	40	50	160
	110	5	15	25	40	45	50	180
	120	5	20	30	40	45	50	195

(1) Depth not exceeding (Metres)	(2) Duration time	21 m	18 m	15 m	12 m	9 m	6 m	3 m	(4) Total time
	11	—	—	—	—	—	—	—	—
	15	—	—	—	—	—	—	5	5
	20	—	—	—	—	—	5	5	10
	25	—	—	—	—	—	5	10	15
	30	—	—	—	—	—	5	20	25
	35	—	—	—	—	5	5	20	30
	Limiting line								
39	40	—	—	—	—	5	10	25	40
	45	—	—	—	5	5	15	30	55
	50	—	—	—	5	5	20	35	65
	55	—	—	—	5	10	25	40	80
	60	—	—	—	5	15	30	45	95
	70	—	—	5	10	20	30	50	115
	75	—	—	5	15	25	40	50	135
	80	—	—	5	20	30	45	50	150
	90	—	5	5	25	40	50	50	170
	100	5	5	15	30	40	45	50	190
	110	5	10	25	30	45	45	50	210
	120	5	15	30	40	45	45	50	230
	9	—	—	—	—	—	—	—	—
	10	—	—	—	—	—	—	5	5
	15	—	—	—	—	—	5	5	10
	20	—	—	—	—	—	5	10	

(1) Depth not exceeding (Metres)	(2) Duration time leaving surface to beginning of ascent not exceeding (min)	(3) Stoppages at different depths (min)								(4) Total time for decompression (min)
		24 m	21 m	18 m	15 m	12 m	9 m	6 m	3 m	
	25		—	—	—	—	—	5	15	20
	30		—	—	—	—	5	5	20	30
	Limiting line									
	35		—	—	—	—	5	10	25	40
	40		—	—	—	5	5	15	30	55
	45		—	—	—	5	10	15	35	65
	50		—	—	—	5	15	20	40	80
	55		—	—	5	5	15	25	45	95
42	60		—	—	5	5	20	35	45	110
	65		—	—	5	10	25	40	45	125
	70		—	—	5	15	30	40	50	140
	75		—	5	5	20	35	45	50	155
	80		—	5	10	20	35	45	50	165
	85		—	5	15	25	40	45	50	180
	95		5	5	20	35	40	45	50	200
	105		5	15	25	35	45	45	60	220
	115		5	20	35	40	45	45	50	240
	8		—	—	—	—	—	—	5	5
	10		—	—	—	—	—	5	5	10
	15		—	—	—	—	—	5	15	20
	20		—	—	—	—	5	5	20	30
	25		—	—	—	—	5	5	20	30
	Limiting line									
	30		—	—	—	—	5	10	25	40
	35		—	—	—	—	5	15	30	50
	40		—	—	—	5	10	15	35	65
45	45		—	—	—	5	15	25	35	80
	50		—	—	5	5	15	25	45	95
	55		—	—	5	10	20	30	50	115
	60		—	—	5	15	25	35	50	130
	65		—	5	5	15	30	40	50	145
	70		—	5	10	20	35	40	50	160
	75		—	5	15	25	35	45	50	175
	80		5	5	20	30	40	45	50	195
	85		5	10	25	35	40	45	50	210
	90		5	15	30	40	45	45	50	230
	10	—	—	—	—	—	—	5	5	10
	15	—	—	—	—	—	—	5	10	15
	20	—	—	—	—	—	5	5	15	25
	25	—	—	—	—	—	5	10	20	35
	Limiting line									
	30	—	—	—	—	5	5	10	25	45
	35	—	—	—	—	5	10	15	30	60
48	40	—	—	—	—	5	10	20	40	75
	45	—	—	—	5	5	15	25	45	95
	50	—	—	—	5	10	20	30	45	110
	55	—	—	—	5	15	25	40	45	130
	60	—	—	5	5	20	25	40	50	145
	65	—	—	5	10	25	35	45	50	165
	70	—	—	5	15	25	40	45	50	180
	75	—	5	5	20	30	40	45	50	195

(1) Depth not exceeding (Metres)	(2) Duration time leaving surface to beginning of ascent not exceeding (min)	(3) Stoppages at different depths (min)								(4) Total time for decompression (min)
		24 m	21 m	18 m	15 m	12 m	9 m	6 m	3 m	
	80		5	10	25	35	40	45	50	210
	85		5	15	30	40	45	45	50	230
	10	—	—	—	—	—	—	5	5	10
	15	—	—	—	—	—	—	5	10	15
	20	—	—	—	—	—	5	5	15	25
	Limiting line									
	25	—	—	—	—	—	5	10	25	40
	30	—	—	—	—	5	5	15	30	55
	35	—	—	—	—	5	10	20	35	70
	40	—	—	—	5	5	15	25	35	85
51	45	—	—	—	5	10	20	30	40	105
	50	—	—	5	5	10	25	35	45	125
	55	—	—	5	5	15	30	40	50	145
	60	—	—	5	10	20	35	45	50	165
	65	—	5	5	15	25	35	45	50	180
	70	—	5	10	15	30	40	45	50	195
	75	—	5	15	20	35	45	45	50	215
	80	5	5	20	35	40	45	45	50	235
	10	—	—	—	—	—	—	5	5	10
	15	—	—	—	—	—	5	5	10	20
	20	—	—	—	—	—	5	10	15	30
	Limiting line									
	25	—	—	—	—	5	5	10	25	45
	30	—	—	—	—	5	10	15	35	65
	35	—	—	—	5	5	15	20	40	85
54	40	—	—	—	5	10	20	25	45	105
	45	—	—	5	5	10	25	35	45	125
	50	—	—	5	5	15	30	40	50	145
	55	—	—	5	10	20	35	45	50	165
	60	—	5	5	15	25	40	45	50	185
	65	—	5	10	20	30	40	45	50	200
	70	—	5	15	25	35	45	45	50	220
	75	5	5	20	30	40	45	45	50	240
	10	—	—	—	—	—	—	5	5	10
	15	—	—	—	—	—	5	5	15	25
	20	—	—	—	—	—	5	10	20	35
	Limiting line									
	25	—	—	—	—	5	5	15	25	50
	30	—	—	—	5	5	10	20	35	75
57	35	—	—	—	5	5	15	30	45	100
	40	—	—	5	5	10	20	35	45	120
	45	—	—	5	5	15	25	40	50	140
	50	—	—	5	10	20	30	45	50	160
	55	—	5	5	15	25	35	45	50	180
	60	—	5	10	20	30	40	45	50	200
	65	5	5	10	25	35	45	45	50	220
	70	5	10	15	30	40	45	45	50	240
	10	—	—	—	—	—	—	5	10	15
	15	—	—	—	—	—	5	5	15	25
	Limiting line									

(1) Depth not exceeding (Metres)	(2) Duration time leaving surface to beginning of ascent not exceeding (min)	(3) Stoppages at different depths (min)								(4) Total time for decompression (min)
		24 m	21 m	18 m	15 m	12 m	9 m	6 m	3 m	
60	20	—	—	—	—	5	5	10	20	40
	25	—	—	—	—	5	10	15	30	60
	30	—	—	—	5	5	15	20	40	85
	35	—	—	—	5	10	20	30	45	110
	40	—	—	5	5	15	25	40	45	135
	45	—	—	5	10	20	30	45	50	160
	50	—	5	5	15	25	35	45	50	180
	55	—	5	10	20	30	40	45	50	200
	60	5	5	10	25	35	45	45	50	220
	65	5	10	15	30	40	45	45	50	240

TABLE 2

RN Air Decompression Tables Non-Metricated

(1) Depth not exceeding (ft)	(2) Duration time leaving surface to beginning of ascent not exceeding (min)	(3) Stoppages at different depths (min)					(4) Total time for decompression (min)
		50 ft	40 ft	30 ft	20 ft	10 ft	
30	No limit	—					
40	135	—	—	—	—	—	—
	165	—	—	—	—	5	5
	195	—	—	—	—	10	10
	225	—	—	—	—	15	15
	255	—	—	—	—	20	20
	330	—	—	—	—	25	25
	390	—	—	—	—	30	30
	660	—	—	—	—	35	35
	Limiting line						
	over 660	—	—	—	—	40	40
50	85	—	—	—	—	—	—
	105	—	—	—	—	5	5
	120	—	—	—	—	10	10
	135	—	—	—	—	15	15
	145	—	—	—	—	20	20
	160	—	—	—	—	25	25
	170	—	—	—	5	25	30
	190	—	—	—	5	30	35
	Limiting line						
	240	—	—	—	10	40	50
	360	—	—	—	30	40	70
	450	—	—	—	35	40	75
	over 450	—	—	—	35	45	80

(1) Depth not exceeding (ft)	(2) Duration time leaving surface to beginning of ascent not exceeding (min)	(3) Stoppages at different depths (min)					(4) Total time for decompression (min)
		50 ft	40 ft	30 ft	20 ft	10 ft	
60	60	—	—	—	—	—	—
	70	—	—	—	—	5	5
	80	—	—	—	5	5	10
	90	—	—	—	5	10	15
	100	—	—	—	5	15	20
	110	—	—	—	5	20	25
	120	—	—	—	5	25	30
	130	—	—	—	5	30	35
	Limiting line						
	140	—	—	—	10	30	40
	150	—	—	—	10	40	50
	160	—	—	—	15	40	55
	180	—	—	—	20	40	60
	200	—	—	5	30	40	75
	255	—	—	10	35	45	90
	325	—	—	20	40	45	105
	395	—	—	35	40	45	120
	over 495	—	—	35	40	50	125
70	40	—	—	—	—	—	—
	55	—	—	—	—	5	5
	60	—	—	—	5	5	10
	70	—	—	—	5	10	15
	75	—	—	—	5	15	20
	85	—	—	—	5	20	25
	90	—	—	—	5	25	30
	95	—	—	5	5	25	35
	Limiting line						
	105	—	—	5	5	35	75
	120	—	—	5	10	40	54
	135	—	—	5	20	45	05
	150	—	—	5	30	45	80
	165	—	—	10	30	50	90
	180	—	—	15	35	50	100
	210	—	—	25	40	50	115
	240	—	5	30	40	50	125
80	30	—	—	—	—	—	—
	40	—	—	—	—	5	5
	50	—	—	—	5	5	10
	55	—	—	—	5	10	15
	60	—	—	—	5	15	20
	70	—	—	—	5	20	25
	75	—	—	—	5	25	30
	Limiting line						
	80	—	—	5	5	30	40
	90	—	—	5	10	35	50
	105	—	—	5	20	40	65
	120	—	5	5	30	45	85
	140	—	5	10	35	50	100
	160	—	10	30	40	50	130
	25	—	—	—	—	—	—
	30	—	—	—	—	5	5
	40	—	—	—	5	5	10

(1) Depth not exceeding (ft)	(2) Duration time leaving surface to beginning of ascent not exceeding (min)	(3) Stoppages at different depths (min)					(4) Total time for decompression (min)
		50 ft	40 ft	30 ft	20 ft	10 ft	
90	45	—	—	—	5	10	15
	50	—	—	—	5	15	20
	55	—	—	—	5	20	25
	60	—	—	5	5	20	30
	65	—	—	5	5	25	35
	Limiting line						
	70	—	—	5	10	30	45
	75	—	—	5	15	30	50
	80	—	—	5	20	35	60
	90	—	—	5	25	40	70
	100	—	—	5	30	45	80
	110	—	5	15	35	45	100
	120	—	5	20	35	50	110
	135	5	5	25	40	50	125
	150	5	10	35	40	50	140
100	20	—	—	—	—	—	—
	25	—	—	—	—	5	5
	30	—	—	—	—	5	10
	35	—	—	—	5	5	10
	35	—	—	—	5	10	15
	40	—	—	—	5	15	20
	45	—	—	—	5	20	25
	50	—	—	5	5	20	30
	55	—	—	5	5	25	35
	Limiting line						
	60	—	—	5	10	30	45
	70	—	—	5	20	35	60
	75	—	5	5	20	40	70
	80	—	5	5	30	40	80
	90	—	5	15	30	45	95
	105	—	5	25	35	50	115
	120	5	10	30	40	50	135

		60 ft	50 ft	40 ft	30 ft	20 ft	10 ft	
110	17	—	—	—	—	—	—	—
	20	—	—	—	—	—	5	5
	25	—	—	—	—	5	5	10
	30	—	—	—	—	5	10	15
	35	—	—	—	—	5	15	20
	40	—	—	—	—	5	20	25
	45	—	—	—	5	5	20	30
	Limiting line							
	50	—	—	—	5	10	25	40
	55	—	—	—	5	15	30	50
	60	—	—	—	5	20	35	60
	65	—	—	5	5	20	40	70
	70	—	—	5	10	20	45	80
	75	—	—	5	15	25	45	90
	80	—	—	5	20	30	45	100
	90	—	5	5	20	40	45	115
	100	—	5	10	25	40	50	130
	110	—	5	20	30	45	50	150
	120	5	5	25	40	45	50	170

(1) Depth not exceeding (ft)	(2) Duration time leaving surface to beginning of ascent not exceeding (min)	(3) Stoppages at different depths (min)						(4) Total time for decompression (min)
		60 ft	50 ft	40 ft	30 ft	20 ft	10 ft	
120	14	—	—	—	—	—	5	—
	20	—	—	—	—	—	5	5
	25	—	—	—	—	5	5	10
	30	—	—	—	—	5	15	20
	35	—	—	—	—	5	20	25
	40	—	—	—	5	5	25	35
	Limiting line							
	45	—	—	—	5	10	25	40
	50	—	—	—	5	15	30	50
	55	—	—	5	5	20	35	65
	60	—	—	5	10	25	40	80
	70	—	—	5	20	30	45	100
	75	—	5	5	20	35	45	110
	80	—	5	10	25	35	45	120
	90	—	5	15	30	40	50	140
	100	5	5	20	35	45	50	160
	110	5	15	25	40	45	50	180
	120	5	20	30	40	45	50	195

(1) Depth not exceeding (ft)	(2) Duration time (min)	70 ft	60 ft	50 ft	40 ft	30 ft	20 ft	10 ft	(4) Total time for decompression (min)
130	11	—	—	—	—	—	—	5	5
	15	—	—	—	—	—	—	5	5
	20	—	—	—	—	—	5	5	10
	25	—	—	—	—	—	5	10	15
	30	—	—	—	—	—	5	20	25
	35	—	—	—	—	5	5	20	30
	Limiting line								
	40	—	—	—	—	5	10	25	40
	45	—	—	—	5	5	15	30	55
	50	—	—	—	5	5	20	35	65
	55	—	—	—	5	10	25	40	80
	60	—	—	—	5	15	30	45	95
130	70	—	—	5	10	20	30	50	115
	75	—	—	5	15	25	40	50	135
	80	—	—	5	20	30	45	50	150
	90	—	5	5	25	40	45	50	170
	100	5	5	15	30	40	45	50	190
	110	5	10	25	35	40	45	50	210
	120	5	15	30	40	45	45	50	230

(1) Depth not exceeding (ft)	(2) Duration time (min)	70 ft	60 ft	50 ft	40 ft	30 ft	20 ft	10 ft	(4) Total time for decompression (min)
140	9	—	—	—	—	—	—	5	5
	10	—	—	—	—	—	—	5	5
	15	—	—	—	—	—	5	5	10
	20	—	—	—	—	—	5	10	15
	25	—	—	—	—	—	5	15	20
	30	—	—	—	—	5	5	20	30
	Limiting line								
	35	—	—	—	—	5	10	25	40
	40	—	—	—	5	5	15	30	55
	45	—	—	—	5	5	20	35	65
	50	—	—	—	5	10	25	40	80
	55	—	—	5	5	15	25	45	95
	60	—	—	5	5	20	35	45	110
	65	—	—	5	10	25	40	45	125

(1) Depth not exceeding (ft)	(2) Duration time leaving surface to beginning of ascent not exceeding (min)	(3) Stoppages at different depths (min)							(4) Total time for decompression (min)
		70 ft	60 ft	50 ft	40 ft	30 ft	20 ft	10 ft	
	70	—	—	5	15	30	40	50	140
	75	—	5	5	20	30	45	50	155
	80	—	5	10	20	35	45	50	165
	85	—	5	15	25	40	45	50	180
	95	5	5	20	34	40	45	50	200
	105	5	15	25	35	45	45	50	220
	115	5	20	35	40	45	45	50	240
	8	—	—	—	—	—	—	—	5
	10	—	—	—	—	—	—	5	5
	15	—	—	—	—	—	5	5	10
	20	—	—	—	—	—	5	15	20
	25	—	—	—	—	5	5	20	30
	Limiting line								
	30	—	—	—	—	5	10	25	40
	35	—	—	—	5	5	10	30	50
	40	—	—	—	5	10	15	35	65
150	45	—	—	—	5	15	20	40	80
	50	—	—	5	5	15	25	45	95
	55	—	—	5	10	20	30	50	115
	60	—	—	5	15	25	35	50	130
	65	—	5	5	15	30	40	50	145
	70	—	5	10	20	30	45	50	160
	75	5	5	15	25	35	45	50	175
	80	5	5	20	30	40	45	50	195
	85	5	10	25	35	40	45	50	210
	90	5	15	30	40	45	45	50	230
	10	—	—	—	—	—	5	5	10
	15	—	—	—	—	—	5	10	15
	20	—	—	—	—	5	5	15	25
	25	—	—	—	—	5	10	20	35
	Limiting line								
	30	—	—	—	5	5	10	25	45
	35	—	—	—	5	10	15	30	60
	40	—	—	—	5	10	20	40	75
160	45	—	—	5	5	15	25	45	95
	50	—	—	5	10	20	30	45	110
	55	—	—	5	15	25	40	45	130
	60	—	5	5	20	25	40	50	145
	65	—	5	10	20	35	45	50	165
	70	—	5	15	25	40	45	50	180
	75	5	5	20	30	40	45	50	195
	80	5	10	25	45	40	45	50	210
	85	5	15	30	40	45	45	50	230

(ft)		80 ft	70 ft	60 ft	50 ft	40 ft	30 ft	20 ft	10 ft	(min)
	10	—	—	—	—	—	—	5	5	10
	15	—	—	—	—	—	—	5	10	15
	20	—	—	—	—	—	5	5	15	25
	Limiting line									
	25	—	—	—	—	—	5	10	25	40
	30	—	—	—	—	5	5	15	30	55

(1) Depth not exceeding (ft)	(2) Duration time leaving surface to beginning of ascent not exceeding (min)	(3) Stoppages at different depths (min)								(4) Total time for decompression (min)
		80 ft	70 ft	60 ft	50 ft	40 ft	30 ft	20 ft	10 ft	
170	35	—	—	—	—	5	10	20	35	70
	40	—	—	—	5	5	15	25	35	85
	45	—	—	—	5	10	20	30	40	105
	50	—	—	5	5	10	25	35	45	125
	55	—	—	5	5	15	30	40	50	145
	60	—	—	5	10	20	35	45	50	165
	65	—	5	5	15	25	35	45	50	180
	70	—	5	10	15	30	40	50	50	195
	75	—	5	15	20	35	45	50	50	215
	80	5	5	20	25	40	45	50	50	235
	10	—	—	—	—	—	—	5	5	10
	15	—	—	—	—	—	5	5	10	20
	20	—	—	—	—	—	5	10	15	30
	Limiting line									
	25	—	—	—	—	5	5	10	25	45
	30	—	—	—	—	5	10	15	35	65
180	35	—	—	—	5	5	15	20	40	85
	40	—	—	—	5	10	20	25	45	105
	45	—	—	5	5	10	25	35	45	125
	50	—	—	5	5	15	30	40	50	145
	55	—	—	5	10	20	35	40	50	165
	60	—	5	5	15	25	40	45	50	185
	65	—	5	10	20	30	40	45	50	200
	70	—	5	15	25	35	45	45	50	220
	75	5	5	20	30	40	45	45	50	240
	10	—	—	—	—	—	—	5	5	10
	15	—	—	—	—	—	5	5	15	25
	20	—	—	—	—	—	5	10	20	35
	Limiting line									
	25	—	—	—	—	5	5	15	25	50
	30	—	—	—	5	5	10	20	35	75
	35	—	—	—	5	5	15	30	45	100
190	40	—	—	5	5	10	20	35	45	120
	45	—	—	5	5	15	25	40	50	140
	50	—	—	5	10	20	30	45	50	160
	55	—	5	5	15	25	35	45	50	180
	60	—	5	10	20	30	40	45	50	200
	65	5	5	10	25	35	45	45	50	220
	70	5	10	15	30	40	45	45	50	240
	10	—	—	—	—	—	—	5	10	15
	15	—	—	—	—	—	5	5	15	25
	Limiting line									
	20	—	—	—	—	5	5	10	20	40
	25	—	—	—	—	5	10	15	30	60
	30	—	—	—	5	5	15	20	40	85
200	35	—	—	5	5	10	20	30	45	110
	40	—	—	5	5	15	25	40	45	735
	45	—	—	5	10	20	30	45	50	160
	50	—	5	5	15	25	35	45	50	180
	55	—	5	10	20	30	40	45	50	200
	60	5	5	10	25	35	45	45	50	220
	65	5	10	15	30	40	45	45	50	240

Appendix B

Diving Facts and Figures

Atmospheric air contains in volume: 78·05 per cent nitrogen, 21·00 per cent oxygen, 1·00 per cent argon, 0·03 per cent carbon dioxide and minute traces of other rare gases.

One atmosphere equals a pressure of 14·7 pounds per square inch, or one bar, or 102 kN/per square metre.

The density of sea water varies according to its salt content, and this varies from place to place. Red Sea water is nearly two pounds (nearly one kilogram) per cubic foot (·0283 metre³) heavier than Baltic water. Fresh water is lighter.

The density of water varies with its temperature, and is greatest at 39 degrees Fahrenheit (4 degrees Centigrade or Celsius).

Boyle's Law relates to gases, and states that 'For a constant temperature, the product of the pressure and the volume of any gas is always constant'. Thus when a mixture of gases is under pressure or compressed, each gas exerts a 'partial' pressure in proportion to its percentage in the mixture—if the pressure or compression is doubled, the pressure of each constituent gas is also doubled.

Archimedes' Principle states that 'When a body is wholly or partially immersed in a fluid, it experiences an upward thrust equal to the weight of the fluid displaced'.

Henry's Law states that 'At a constant temperature, the amount of a gas which dissolves in a liquid with which it is in contact, is proportional to the partial pressure of that gas'.

Conversions

1 fathom = 6 feet or 1·828 metres.

1 nautical mile = 6,080 feet or 1·853 kilometres.

1 knot = a speed of one nautical mile per hour.

Water depth (feet) to atmospheres or bars—divide by 33.

Water depth (metres) to atmospheres or bars—divide by 10.

One cubic foot (0·0283 m³) of salt water weighs 64 lbs (29·4 kg).

One cubic foot (0·0283 m³) of fresh water weighs 62·5 lbs (28·3 kg).

One atmosphere = one bar = 14·7 psi = 102 kN/per square metre.

Appendix C

Additional Reading

Although not exhaustive, the following lists contain books and magazines that I have found informative or entertaining.

Books

Technique
National Association of Underwater Instructors Handbook (NAUI)
BSAC Diving Manual (BSAC)
Diving Officer's Handbook, G. Skuse (ed.), (BSAC)
F. Waterman, *Swimming*, (Teach Yourself Books)
B. Allen (ed. G. Cherry), *Skin Diving and Snorkeling*, (A & C Black)
Vane Ivanovich, *Modern Spearfishing*, (Kaye & Ward)
Leo Zanelli, *Advanced Underwater Swimming*, (Kaye & Ward)
Illustrated Handbook of Life Saving Instruction, (Royal Life Saving Society)
Decompression and Narcosis, (Scottish Sub-Aqua Club)
New Science of Skin and Scuba Diving, (Darton, Longman & Todd)
Diving Instructors & Examiners Handbook, (Irish Underwater Council)

Wrecks and Treasure
Leo Zanelli, *Shipwrecks Around Britain*, (Kaye & Ward)

Leo Zanelli, *Unknown Shipwrecks Around Britain*, (Kaye & Ward)

Undersea Treasures, (National Geographic Society)

Bruce D. Berman, *Encyclopedia of American Shipwrecks*, (Mariners Press)

W. Ratigan, *Great Lakes Shipwrecks and Survivals*, (Eerdmans)

Kendall McDonald, *The Wreck Detectives*, (Harrup)

Clay Blair, *Diving For Treasure*, (Arthur Barker)

A. C. Clarke, *The Treasure of the Great Reef*, (Arthur Barker)

Wagner & Taylor, *Pieces of Eight*, (Longmans)

Robert Stenuit, *Treasures of the Armada*, (David & Charles)

Alexander McKee, *Mary Rose*, (Souvenir Press)

Peter Marsden, *The Wreck of the Amsterdam*, (Hutchinson)

R. Burgess, *Sinkings, Salvages and Shipwrecks*, (American Heritage Press)

Paul Johnstone, *The Archaeology of Ships*, (Bodley Head)

Buried & Sunken Treasure, (Marshall Cavendish)

Cornish/Devon/North Wales Shipwrecks, (series of books, David & Charles)

Godfrey & Lassey, *Yorkshire Wrecks*, (Dalesman)

S. C. George, *Jutland to Junkyard*, (Patrick Stevens)

General:

Leo Zanelli (ed.), *The Subaqua Guide*, (Subaqua Magazine)

Russell & Yong, *The Seas*, (Warne)

G. E. R. Deacon (ed.), *Oceans*, (Paul Hamlyn)

The Sea, (Life Nature Library)

Capt. W. B. Gray, *Creatures of the Sea*, (Muller)

Haas & Knorr, *Seashore*, (Burke)

Kosch & Frierling & Janus, *Marine Life*, (Burke)

C. P. Idyll, *Abyss*, (Constable)

Helen Raitt, *Exploring the Deep Pacific*, (Staples)

Englehardt, *Pond-life*, (Burke)

Sir R. H. Davis, *Deep Diving & Submarine Operations*, (Saint Catherine Press)

Desmond Young, *The Man in the Helmet*, (Cassell)

J. Cousteau, *The Silent World*, (Hamish Hamilton)

Houot & Willm, 2000 *Fathoms Down*, (Hamish Hamilton & Hart-Davis)

Waldron & Gleeson, *The Frogmen*, (Evans)

Hans Hass, *To Unplumbed Depths*, (Harrup)

Lotte Hass, *Girl on the Ocean Floor*, (Harrup)

Alexander McKee, *History Under the Sea*, (Hutchinson)

J. Cousteau, *The Ocean World of Jacques Cousteau*, (series of books; World/Angus & Robertson)

Paul Johnstone, *The Archaeology of Ships*, (Bodley Head)

J. Cousteau, *The Undersea Discoveries of Jacques-Yves Cousteau*, (series: Cassell)

Jacques Piccard, *The Sun Beneath the Sea*, (Hale)

Susan Schlee, *A History of Oceanography*, (Hale)

J. B. Sweeney, *Pictorial History of Oceanographic Submersibles*, (Hale)

A. Major, *Collecting World Sea Shells*, (Bartholomew)

Underwater Photography:

Jim & Cathy Church, *Beginning Underwater Photography*, (J&C Church)

Jerry Greenberg, *Underwater Photography Simplified*, (Seahawk Press)

Schenck & Kendall, *Underwater Photography*, (Cornell Maritime Press)

Rebikoff & Cherney, *Underwater Photography*, (Chilton Books)

E. R. Cross, *Underwater Photography & Television*, (Exposition Press, 1954)

H. Dobbs, *Underwater Photography*, (Focal Press)

Magazines

United States:
Skin Diver, 8490 Sunset Blvd., Los Angeles, California 90069.
National Geographic, Washington D.C. (Although this subscription magazine does not always contain underwater features, when they do appear they are superb).

Great Britain:
SubAqua Magazine, 28 Southampton St., London WC2.
Scottish Diver, 2 Kirklee Circus, Glasgow G12 0TW.
Triton, 40 Grays Inn Road, London WC1X 8LR.

New Zealand:
Dive, P.O. Box 20, Whangarei.

Germany:
Der Taucher, 7000 Stuttgart-50, Dennerstrasse 58.
Submarin, Heering-Verlag GmbH, 8 München 70.

Italy:
Mondo Sommerso, Messaggerie Internazionale, Via Visconti di Modrone, 1, Milano.

Appendix D

Metrication

For convenience, the measurements, weights and pressures in this book are quoted, where possible, in a dual manner e.g. 33 ft (10 m) imperial/metric. But whatever system you prefer, I must stress the importance of learning the metric system and 'thinking metric'. This is not just because I personally think the metric system is best for divers, but because over 90% of the world has adopted metrication, and the rest *must* follow. However, the process is not a simple adaptation because many units or terms are not as yet standardized. For example the pressure of one atmosphere is called a 'bar' or 102 kN/per square metre—depending on your geographical location and the opinion of the local ruling diving authority. So this appendix is no more than a guide. In fact this whole book has been written, in this context, for ease of understanding, which is why units and terms are often entered in the most simple manner—it is far easier to visualize 1 atmosphere than 14·7 psi or 102 kN.

Metrication has particular advantages for the diver. For instance, 1 atmosphere of pressure is equal to a depth of 33 ft underwater or, in metric terms, 10 m. Thus we have a progression, in unwieldy imperial measurements, such as that outlined on following page. Compare it with the metric version.

The metric system, in this case, is absurdly simple and is obviously so much easier to remember than the imperial.

Imperial	*Metric*
1 at = 33 ft	1 at = 10 m
2 at = 66 ft	2 at = 20 m
3 at = 99 ft	3 at = 30 m
4 at = 132 ft	4 at = 40 m
5 at = 165 ft	5 at = 50 m

In some countries the atmosphere (at) as a unit has been replaced by the bar (b) as a unit of gas pressure. But as the bar is, for all *practical* purposes equal to one atmosphere, they can be virtually interchanged, and you might see tables like the following:

1 bar = 10 m	1 b = 10 m
2 bar = 20 m	2 b = 20 m
3 bar = 30 m	3 b = 30 m etc.

How about cylinder capacities? This is not too difficult for divers who have read most of the advertising. Volumes have previously been quoted in cubic feet (ft³) and will now be generally measured in cubic metres (m³). However the cubic metre is quite a large volume and the unit in common for cylinder capacity is the litre. The following table illustrates some more of the advantages of the metric system:

Cylinder Capacity Comparisons

Cubic feet	*Litres*	*Cubic metres*
40	1132	1·132
50	1415	1·415
60	1699	1·699
70	1982	1·982

Notice the ease with which the capacity in litres is equated with the capacity in cubic metres—the decimal point is merely inserted one hundred (three places) from the end. Try to do the same thing as quickly by equating 40 cubic feet with cubic yards!

Regarding temperature, many of us are acquainted with the metric Centigrade system, as opposed to Fahrenheit.

But you will see a new name—Celsius—crop up. Don't worry too much about this because it is only a new name for Centigrade. Centigrade is a different unit of measurement in some countries so the name Celsius has been adopted instead.

Temperature

Fahrenheit	*Celsius/Centigrade*
212 (boiling)	100
100	37·8
86	30
68	20
50	10
41	5
32 (freezing	0

Here again we have a rational yardstick. Freezing is indicated by zero, and boiling point as 100. Both, incidentally, for water, not alcohol or milk!

The metric unit of length is the metre. This is easier to visualize if you remember that it is roughly one yard. For the fussy diver, one metre equals 3·28 ft; alternatively, one yard or three feet equals 0·914 metre. The smallest unit of length that we are likely to use is the millimetre (mm), which is one thousandth of a metre, and the centimetres (cm), which is one hundredth.

The secret of a quick changeover to metrication is to forget the old measurements and 'think metric'. If you try to ignore metrication, it will take years to get the hang of it, but if you try to forget the old system and think metric, you will soon get the hang of it. A knowledge of metrication is far more important to the diver than it is to most people; most diving manuals have already gone metric, as have the nautical charts of virtually every navy and hydrographic department in the world.

Appendix E

Beaufort Wind Scale

Beaufort International number	Wind	As used by Mariners		Indications at sea
		Units of Speed		
		Nautical miles per hours (knots)	Feet per second	
0	Calm	Less than 1	Less than 2	Sea mirror smooth
1	Light air	1–3	2–5	Small wavelets like scales, no foam crests
2	Light breeze	4–6	6–11	Waves short and more pronounced; crests begin to break; foam has glassy appearance — not yet white
3	Gentle breeze	7–10	12–18	
4	Moderate breeze	11–16	19–27	Waves are longer; many white horses
5	Fresh breeze	17–21	28–36	Waves now pronounced and long; white foam crests everywhere
6	Strong breeze	22–27	37–46	Larger waves form; white foam crests more extensive
7	Strong wind	28–33	47–56	Sea heaps up; wind starts to blow the foam in streaks
8	Fresh gale	34–40	57–68	Height of waves increases visibly; also height of crests; much foam is blown in dense streaks
9	Strong gale	41–47	69–80	
10	Whole gale	48–55	81–93	High waves with long overhanging crests; great foam patches
11	Storm	56–65	94–110	Waves so high that ships within sight are hidden in the troughs; sea covered with streaky foam; air filled with spray.
12	Hurricane	Above 65	Above 110	

Beaufort International number	As used by Landsmen		
	Wind	Unit of Speed — Statute m.p.h. recorded at 33ft. above ground level	Indications on land
0	Calm	Less than 1	Smoke rises vertically.
1	Light air	1–3	Direction shown by smoke but not by wind vanes.
2	Light breeze	4–7	Wind felt on face; leaves rustle, ordinary vanes moved by wind.
3	Gentle breeze	8–12	Leaves and small twigs in constant motion; wind extends light flag.
4	Moderate breeze	13–18	Raises dust and waste paper; small branches are moved.
5	Fresh breeze	19–24	Small trees in leaf begin to sway; crested wavelets form on inland waters.
6	Strong breeze	25–31	Large branches in motion; whistling heard in telegraph wires; umbrellas used with difficulty.
7	Moderate gale (see note)	32–38	Whole trees in motion; inconvenience felt when walking against wind.
8	Fresh gale	39–46	Breaks twigs off trees; greatly impedes progress.
9	Strong gale	47–54	Slight structural damage occurs (chimney pots and slates removed).
10	Whole gale	55–63	Seldom experienced inland; trees uprooted; considerable structural damage occurs.
11	Storm	64–75	Very rarely experienced; accompanied by widespread damage.
12	Hurricane	Above 75	—

Note: Mariners never use the term 'Gale' for winds of less than Force 8. Gale warnings are only issued and cones hoisted for winds of Force 8 upwards.

Index

TEACH YOURSELF BOOKS

COARSE ANGLING

Cliff Parker

Written by a well-known coarse angling expert, this book
is designed to show the beginner how to fish successfully
from the start, and the experienced angler how to catch
more fish.

The book covers each species chapter by chapter,
describing their locality, feeding habits and behaviour,
along with how to fish them using the appropriate tackle,
baits and methods.

Packed with tips and information, this is the ideal book
both to get the novice off to a good start and to increase the
'old hand's' skill.

UNITED KINGDOM	£1.75
AUSTRALIA	$5.65*
NEW ZEALAND	$5.50

ISBN 0 340 20381 1   *recommended but not obligatory

TEACH YOURSELF BOOKS

SEA ANGLING

Trevor Housby

Written by a well-known sea angling expert, this book is
designed to show the beginner how to fish successfully from
the start, and the experienced angler how to catch more
fish.

The book covers each species chapter by chapter, describing
their locality, feeding habits and behaviour, along with how
to fish them using the appropriate tackle, baits and
methods.

Packed with tips and information, this is the ideal book
both to get the novice off to a good start and to increase the
'old hand's' skill.

UNITED KINGDOM	£1.25*
AUSTRALIA	$3.93*
NEW ZEALAND	$3.95
CANADA	$4.95

ISBN 0 340 20378 1   *recommended but not obligatory

TEACH YOURSELF BOOKS

FLY FISHING

Maurice Wiggin

Many people are convinced that fly fishing is so complicated and difficult that you need years of study and expert tuition to master it. This is quite untrue. If you study this book and use your common sense, you should become a reasonably proficient fly fisherman in your first season.

The object of this book is to encourage novices to take up their rods with confidence and boldness. It covers every stage and technique of fly fishing, from building a rod through casting the fly to the grassing of the fish. And the enthusiasm of the author, a well-known columnist on a national newspaper, is as delightful and instructive as is his encyclopaedic knowledge.

UNITED KINGDOM	95p
AUSTRALIA	$3.05*
NEW ZEALAND	$3.05
CANADA	$3.05

ISBN 0 340 16677 0   *recommended but not obligatory

TEACH YOURSELF BOOKS

SQUASH

Leslie Hamer & Rex Bellamy

Squash, perhaps the ideal sport for the modern desk-bound
city-dweller with little time for exercise, has never been more
popular than it is today.

This book, written by two of the game's most distinguished
figures, fills the need for a comprehensive guide to the game;
its past, present and future, and the strokes and tactics
necessary if players at all levels are to enjoy it to the full.

Now in a new updated edition, the readable and lucid
text covers every aspect of the game, from equipment, the
rules and the various grips and shots that may be used, to
match play, court language and etiquette, and general hints
on fitness and practice.

UNITED KINGDOM	75p
AUSTRALIA	$2.45*
NEW ZEALAND	$2.40
CANADA	$2.50

ISBN 0 340 20745 0   *recommended but not obligatory